Series: *Language, Media & Education Studies*

Edited by: Marcel Danesi & Leonard G. Sbrocchi

INTERPRETING
ADVERTISEMENTS

A Semiotic Guide

by

Marcel Danesi

LEGAS

New York   Ottawa   Toronto

Canadian Cataloguing in Publication Data

Danesi, Marcel,
   Interpreting advertisements: a semiotic guide

(Language, media & education studies ; 1)
Includes bibliographical references.
ISBN 0-921252-35-8

   1. Advertising.   2. Semiotics.   I. Title.   II. Series.

HF5822.D35   302.23   C95-900795-4

For further information about the series and for orders:

LEGAS

P.O.Box 040328	68 Kamloops Ave.	2908 Dufferin St.
Brooklyn, N.Y.	Ottawa, Ontario	Toronto, Ontario
11204-002	K1V 7C9	M6B 3S8

Printed and bound in Canada

CONTENTS

PREFACE

Everywhere one turns these days, one is bound to come upon an advertisement of some kind: on billboards, on the radio, on television, on buses and subways, in magazines and newspapers, on flyers in the mail, on clothes, shoes, hats, pens, and the list could go on and on. To say that *advertising* has become the twentieth century's most ubiquitous means of mass communication is an understatement. Using both verbal and nonverbal symbols to make its messages, it has become an integral part of modern-day social discourse. As Leiss, Kline & Jhally (1990: 1) aptly remark, "in industrial societies in this century, national consumer product advertising has become one of the great vehicles of social communication."

Advertising imbues and defines the contemporary psyche. At one level, the advertiser's implicit messages, styles of presentation, and visual images are surreptitiously shaping the thoughts, personalities, and lifestyle behaviors of countless individuals, as well as covertly suggesting how we can best satisfy our innermost urges and aspirations. But at another level, advertising has evolved into a *fin du siècle* medium of artistic expression, tapping into the one trait that distinguishes the human species from all others — the capacity and urgent propensity to *make* meaning through symbolism. In my opinion, understanding how advertising does this has now become crucial, especially if late twentieth-century humans are to retain their autonomy and selfhood in a world bent on pressuring everyone to conform to, and to strive for, mass hedonistic values. Like never before has Zeus's warning to Narcissus, "Watch thineself," been so portentous and relevant.

This is not a critical book on advertising, although it does reflect some of my own critical thoughts on the topic (especially in the final chapter). There are many excellent works currently on the market that look at advertising critically that the reader can consult. Nor is it designed to be a comprehensive, indepth analysis of the advertising code. It is intended as a practical guide on how to decode the underlying messages and meanings woven into many current advertising texts that promote lifestyle products. The decoding approach employed, discussed, and illustrated throughout, is that of *semiotic* analysis. This book is, therefore, directed both towards a general audience and to students taking introductory courses in such areas as semiotics, communication theory, media studies, psychology, and culture studies. I have written it so that as broad an audience as possible can appreciate and understand, in a clear and general way, how semiotic inquiry can be applied to understand the many lifestyle advertisements we see on a daily basis. For this reason, both the presentational style and contents of the book are designed specifically for those without prior technical knowledge of the field. A convenient glossary of technical terms is included at the end. I have made every attempt possible to build upon what the reader, in my view, already knows intuitively about *semiotics*, the science that studies how humans go about making their messages. There is perhaps no other domain of application like advertising that best shows the power of semiotics as a "science of interpretation." So, in a basic sense, this manual constitutes a brief, "user-friendly" introduction to *semiotics* itself. It is designed to illustrate how semiotic notions can be applied to understanding lifestyle advertising — a code rendered highly persuasive through the power of *connotation*.

The simple plan of this manual is as follows. The opening chapter provides an overview both of advertising and of the primary notions and concepts that characterize the discipline of semiotics as it is practised today. The second chapter describes and illustrates how the basic concepts of semiotic analysis can be employed to decode magazine ads and television commercials. The third and fourth chapters then go into more detail respectively into the nature of the iconic and the verbal features that make lifestyle advertisements particularly appealing and compelling. The final chapter constitutes my own reflections on the relation between advertising and contemporary culture.

I must warn the reader that the theoretical stances put forward and the analytical techniques illustrated throughout this manual reflect my own approach to semiotics and my own interpretations of specific advertisements. The presence of the "author in the text" is unavoidable. But whether the reader agrees or disagrees with any of my semiotic analyses is besides the point of this manual. My hope is simply that this book will induce a critical perspective on advertising that he or she might not have had previously. In my view, that and that alone, will have made the writing of this book worth the while.

I wish to thank the editorial staff at *Legas* for all their advice, support, and expert help. I am especially grateful to Professor Leonard G. Sbrocchi, who encouraged me to share my particular approach to semiotics with a larger public by starting a series with Legas of practically-focused manuals and by suggesting that I write the first volume for the series. I must also thank Victoria College of the University of Toronto for having allowed me the privilege of teaching in, and coordinating, its *Program in Semiotics* over the past seven years. And I must not forget to thank the many students I have taught over the years for their encouragement, critical insights, and constant enthusiasm. I would like especially to thank Adriana De Marco, Janet Winger, Marcus Sagar, Mina Wallin, and Sandy Di Martino for allowing me to incorporate aspects of their own analytical perspectives into my discussion of some of the ads examined in this book. Any infelicities that this book might contain are my sole responsibility. To all who read this book, I hope that the age-old warning *caveat emptor* ("let the buyer beware") will come to have a much more specific meaning.

Marcel Danesi
Victoria College, 1995

1

ADVERTISING AND SEMIOTIC ANALYSIS

Introduction

The term *advertising* derives from the medieval Latin verb *advertere* "to direct one's attention to." It designates any type or form of public announcement intended to promote the sale of specific commodities or services. Advertising is to be distinguished from other materials and activities aimed at swaying and influencing opinions, attitudes, and behaviors such as *propaganda, publicity,* and *public relations.Propaganda* refers to any systematic dissemination of doctrines, views, beliefs, etc. reflecting specific interests and ideologies (political, social, philosophical, etc.). *Publicity* refers to the craft of disseminating any information that concerns a person, group, event, or product through some form of public media. *Public relations* is the term commonly used to refer to the activities and techniques deployed by organizations and individuals to establish favorable attitudes and responses in their behalf on the part of the general public or of special groups.

Advertising is an integral component of contemporary urban, industrialized societies. In this century, it has evolved into a form of persuasive message-making that is designed to influence how we perceive and identify a product, a service, an organization, etc. Advertising techniques range in complexity from simple notices in the classified sections of newspapers and magazines to sophisticated magazine lifestyle ads and television commercials. Since the sixties advertising campaigns have also been mounted and directed toward issues of social concern (cancer, AIDS, human rights, po-verty, etc.). But in this book I shall be concerned exclusively with the commercial uses of advertising, since the kinds of messages forged in that domain have come to have a prominent place in contemporary mass communications. In modern industrialized societies commercial advertising has become a kind of "privileged" discourse that has replaced, by and large, more traditional forms of discourse — sermons, political oratory, proverbs, wise sayings, etc. — which in

(Leiss, Kline & Jhally 1990: 1). Advertising exalts and inculcates Epicurean values that are reflective of a consumerist world which sees human beings more and more each day as "recurrent units" that can be classified indistinguishably into "taste cultures," "lifestyle groups," "market segments," etc. and that can, therefore, be understood, managed, and manipulated by the laws of statistics. As the great psychoanalyst Carl Gustav Jung (1957: 19-20) warned several decades ago, we live indeed in an age which dangerously views a human being as a unit in an assemblage, rather than as "something unique and singular which in the last analysis can neither be known nor compared with anything else."

Advertising falls into two main categories: (1) *consumer advertising*, which is directed towards the promotion of some product, and (2) *trade advertising*, in which a sales pitch is made to dealers and professionals through appropriate trade publications and media. The focus of this book is on the former, which can be defined more specifically as any text "designed to spread information with a view to promoting the sales of marketable goods and services" (Harris & Seldon 1962: 40). Consumer advertising, incidentally, gave birth to the first agency for recording and analyzing data on advertising effectiveness in 1914 with the establishment of the Audit Bureau of Circulations in the United States, an independent organization founded and supported by newspaper and magazine publishers wishing to obtain circulation statistics and to standardize the ways of presenting them. Then, in 1936 the Advertising Research Foundation was established to conduct research on, and to develop, advertising techniques with the capacity to enhance the authenticity, reliability, efficiency, and usefulness of all advertising and marketing research. Today, the increasing sophistication with statistical information-gathering techniques makes it possible for advertisers to target audiences on the basis of where people live, what income they make, what educational background they have, etc. in order to determine their susceptibility to, or inclination towards, certain products.

Advertising messages are now communicated through all media (print, video and television, radio), in all kinds of contexts (shop windows, billboards, fliers, etc.), and by means of various modes of transmission (airplane skywriting, delivery trucks, etc.). There are even television channels, magazines, and other media that are exclusively concerned with advertising (e.g.*The Shopping Network, Eaton's Catalogue*, etc.).

This chapter has a twofold purpose: (1) to sketch a history of advertising as a backdrop to the discussion that will ensue, and (2) to introduce some basic notions in semiotic analysis. The reader who is desirous of more in-depth treatments of, or perspectives on, the history of advertising can consult the following works: Elliott (1962), Harris & Seldon (1962), Presbrey (1968), Hindley & Hindley (1972), Heighton & Cunningham (1976), Pollay (1979), Albion & Farris (1981), Pope (1983), Driver & Foxall (1984), Fox (1984), Marchand (1985). The reader interested in reading something more comprehensive introducing semiotic theory and practice can consult the following texts: Barthes (1968), Sebeok (1976, 1979, 1981, 1986, 1991), Eco (1976), Hawkes (1977), McCannell & McCannell (1982), Berger (1984), Solomon (1988), Frutiger (1989), Nöth (1990), Danesi (1994).

Advertising: An Historical Sketch

Perhaps no other twentieth-century form of communication has caused as much controversy as has advertising. In the last few decades it has generated a truly bitter debate in society at large: Does it influence attitudes and behavior? Is it a valuable contributor to the efficiency of a free market economy? Is it a form of artistic expression (note that every year at the Cannes film festival prizes are awarded in the field of advertising)? Such questions have led to a spate of studies which have examined advertising from the broader psychological and cultural perspectives that such questions presuppose. Perhaps the starting point of the debate can be traced to the publication of Vance Packard's 1957 work on the subliminal effects of advertising, *The Hidden Persuaders*, which inspired an outpouring of studies in the seventies, eighties, and early nineties examining the effects of advertising on individuals and on society at large (e.g. Inglis 1972, Key 1972, 1976, 1980, 1988, Leymore 1975, Ewen 1976, 1988, Barnouw 1978, Rotzoll, Haefner & Sandage 1976, Atwan 1979, Goffman 1979, Courtenoy & Whipple 1983, Anderson 1984, Schudson 1984, Singer 1986, Jhally 1987, Sinclair 1987, Barthel 1988, McCracken 1988, Moog 1990, Leiss, Kline & Jhally 1990, Wernick 1991, Danna 1992, Vardar 1992). Advertising has also been the target of numerous major analytical, critical, and technical investigations over the same time period (e.g. Fowles 1976, Andren, Ericsson, Ohlsson & Tännsjö 1978, Dyer 1982, Vestergaard & Schrøder 1985, Williamson 1985). The question that most of the studies have entertained, without answering in any definitive fashion, is whether advertising has become a force molding cultural mores and individual behaviors or whether it constitutes no more than a "mirror" of deeper cultural tendencies within urbanized, industrialized societies. Without going into the debate here, suffice it to say that there is one thing with which virtually everyone agrees — advertising has become one of the most recognizable and appealing forms of aesthetic communication to which virtually everyone in society is exposed. The images and messages that advertisers promulgate on a daily basis delineate the contemporary social landscape.

But to what extent are the warnings contained in research papers and monographs on the effects advertising purportedly has on society accurate or justified? Is advertising to be blamed for causing virtually everything, from obesity to street violence? Are media moguls the shapers of behavior that so many would claim they are today? Has advertising spawned the contemporary world? Are the victims of media, as Key (1989: 13) suggests, people who "scream and shout hysterically at rock concerts and later in life at religious revival meetings?" There is no doubt that media artifacts probably play some role in shaping some behaviors in some individuals. The highly inflated amount of consumption of fast foods, tobacco, alcohol, and other media-hyped substances is probably related somewhat to the slick promotion ploys utilized by magazine ads and television commercials. But, in my view, even though people mindlessly absorb the messages promulgated constantly by advertisements, and although these may have some subliminal effects on behavior, we accept media images, by and large, only if they suit our already-established preferences. It is more accurate to say that advertising produces images that reinforce already-forged lifestyle models in individuals. Advertisers are not innovators. They are more intent on reinforcing lifestyle behaviors than in spreading commercially-risky innovations. Advertisements are not in themselves disruptive of the value systems of the cultural mainstream; rather, they reflect "shifts" already present in popular culture. If they are indeed psychologically effective, then, as will be argued throughout this book, it is primarily because they tap into deeply-engrained mythical and metaphorical structures that constitute a culture.

It may come as a surprise to discover that advertising is over 3,000 years old! A poster found by archeologists in Thebes in 1,000 B. C. is thought to be a relic of one of the world's first ads. In large letters it offered a whole gold coin for the capture of a runaway slave. Similar kinds of posters have been found by archeologists scattered throughout ancient societies. An outdoor advertisement found among the ruins of ancient Rome offers property for rent; another found painted on a wall in Pompeii calls the attention of travelers to a tavern located in a different town.

In medieval times there emerged a widespread form of oral advertising. That was the era in which so-called town "criers" read public notices aloud, being employed by merchants to make known and to promote their wares. Town criers were the forerunners of modern television announcers. It would seem that throughout history advertising in marketplaces and temples has constituted a popular means of disseminating information and of promoting the barter and sale of goods.

The dawn of the modern era of advertising can be traced to the fifteenth century when Johann Gutenberg (1400?-1468?), the inventor of movable type, made the printed word an accessible mode of mass communication. After the "Gutenberg revolution" fliers and posters could be printed easily and posted in public places or inserted in books, pamphlets, newspapers, etc. By the latter part of the seventeenth century, when newspapers were beginning to circulate widely, print advertising became an omnipresent format for the promotion of products and services. The *London Gazette* became the first newspaper to reserve even a section exclusively for advertising. So successful was this venture that by the end of the century several agencies came into being for the specific purpose of creating newspaper ads for merchants and artisans.

The ads inserted in newspapers and magazines in the seventeenth century were printed and laid out like modern classifieds, without illustrative support; but they nonetheless had all the persuasive verbal flavor of their contemporary descendants. They catered to the wealthy clients who bought and read newspapers, promoting the sale of tea, coffee, wigs, books, theater tickets, and the like. Dyer (1982: 16-17) cites a very modern-sounding advertisement for toothpaste that dates back to 1660 England:

> Most excellent and proved Dentifrice to scour and cleanse the Teeth, making them white as ivory, preserves the Tooth-ach; so that being constantly used, the Parties using it are never troubled with the Tooth-ach. It fastens the Teeth, sweetens the Breath, and preserves the Gums and Mouth from cankers and Impothumes…and the right are only to be had at Thomas Rookes, Stationer.

Advertising spread rapidly throughout the eighteenth century, proliferating to the point that the writer and lexicographer Samuel Johnson (1709-1784) felt impelled to make the following statement in *The Idler:* "Advertisements are now so numerous that they are very negligently perused, and it is therefore become necessary to gain attention by magnificence of promise and by eloquence sometimes sublime and sometimes pathetic" (quoted in Panati 1984: 168). Ad creators were starting to pay more attention to the design and layout of the ad text. The syntactically cumbersome and lugubrious texts of the previous century were being replaced more and more by words set out in blocks, by shorter sentences, and by contrasting type fonts. The art of coining and inventing new language to fit the ad text was becoming a daily reality. Advertising was seemingly starting to change the ideational texture of language and society. Everything from clothes to beverages were being promoted through ingenious new forms of print advertising: by repetitions of the firm's name or product, by phrases set in eye-catching patterns, by contrasting font styles and formats, by the deployment of effective visual techniques, and by the creation of slogans and neologisms. As the nineteenth century came to a close, American advertisers in particular, as Dyer (1982: 32) points out, were using "more colloquial, personal and informal language to address the customer" and also exploiting "the uses of humour to attract attention to a product."

The nineteenth century saw the appearance and institutionalization of the advertising agency. By the turn of the present century, such agencies had become themselves large business enterprises, constantly developing new techniques and methods to get people to think of themselves as "market units" rather than as individuals or as a public. The following advice, given by one of the early advertising agents — a man named Claude Hopkins — to prospective ad copywriters in the early part of this century, is typical of the emerging mindset in marketing (quoted in Bendinger 1988: 14)

> Don't think of people in the mass. That gives you a blurred view. Think of a typical individual, man or woman, who is likely to want what you sell. The advertising man studies the consumer. He tries to place himself in the position of the buyer. His success largely depends on doing that to the exclusion of everything else.

Throughout this century advertising has focused on promoting and ensconcing consumerism as a way of life. It now constitutes a form of aesthetic communication that proposes marketplace solutions to virtually all our social problems. We live in a culture, seemingly, that views shopping as much more than just acquiring the essentials required for daily living. It is becoming more and more an end in itself. No wonder, then, that the shopping malls are filled with thrill-seekers who would otherwise become stir crazy. Perhaps, as many social critics warn, we do indeed live in a world conjured up by lifestyle ads and TV commercials. Stuart Ewen (1988: 20) puts it eloquently in the following manner:

> If the "life-style" of style is not realizable in life, it is nevertheless the most constantly available lexicon from which many of us draw the visual grammar of our lives. It is a behavioral model that is closely interwoven with modern patterns of survival and desire. It is a hard to define but easy to recognize element in our current history.

The emergence of our "ad-mediated world," as some critics denominate it, occurred in the decades between 1890 and the 1920's when industrial corporations grew into the mammoth structures that they are today, transforming the workplace into a mechanized, automatonic system of mass production. At that point in time advertising became a crucial medium not just for informing people about the availability and qualities of goods, but also for restructuring perceptions of lifestyle behaviors that could be associated with the acquisition of specific products. Business and aesthetics had obviously joined forces by the first decades of this century. From the twenties onward, advertising agencies began to broaden their approaches, attempting more and more to build an unbroken, imagistic bridge between the product and the consumer's consciousness. Everything from product name, design, and packaging, to the creation of lifestyle moods now fall within the purview of the craft of advertising.

By the thirties, advertising messages moved away from describing the product to focusing on the consumer of the product. Themes such as family, status, authority, etc. came to be used as the threads with which to weave together advertising texts. By the fifties, advertising started to move away slightly from the consumer as primary target, moving more towards creating product imagery with which the consumer could identify (Woodward & Denton 1988: 192). Since the sixties, advertising has gone a few steps further. Advertisers are now creating ads and commercials which, below their surface, tap into unconscious desires, urges, and mythic motifs embedded in the human psyche.

At a broad cultural level, the constant surface messages coming out of ads and commercials offer the kind of hope to which religions and social philosophies once held exclusive rights — security against the hazards of old age, better positions in life, popularity and personal prestige, social advancement, better health, happiness, etc. The modern advertiser stresses not the product, but the benefits that may be expected from its purchase. And, as we shall see in subsequent chapters, the advertiser is becoming more and more successful at setting foot into the same subconscious regions of psychic experience which were once explored only by philosophers, artists, and religious thinkers.

It is interesting to note, parenthetically, that advertising is now one of the most strictly regulated industries in North America. This bears witness, no doubt, to the perception that it has become indeed a potent form of persuasion. As a consequence, advertisers now have to prepare different versions of an advertisement to comply with varying state and provincial laws.

Advertisers obviously are aware that the contemporary consumer has an insatiable desire for pleasure. More and more, their techniques seem to be designed to speak indirectly to the unconscious level of mind where the Freudian *Id*— the unconscious part of the psyche actuated by fundamental impulses toward fulfilling instinctual needs — can be aroused unwittingly. The sense of touch and smell, which are largely downplayed in our culture, are frequently evoked in an ad text through synesthesia — as we shall see in a subsequent chapter — so as to induce an unconscious desire for the product by sensory association. As Freudian psychoanalysis has always emphasized, any one of the unconscious tendencies that a culture represses systematically can be manipulated and actuated easily by suasion techniques into motivating forces and drives. More will be said about this in the next chapter.

In this world of image and style, there is an incessant need for change, for new objects of consumption. The semiotician Roland Barthes (1967) referred to this restlessness and madness for constant novelty as "neomania." Obsolescence is, in fact, regularly built into a product, so that the same product can be sold again and again under new guises.

All the glitz and imagery of ads and commercials yell out one promise to all: "Buy this or that and you will not be bored; you will be *happy* or *cool*." The sad truth is that what we call happiness cannot be bought. We are living in a very unstable world which puts much more of a premium on satisfying consumerist urges than it does on the attainment of spirituality and wisdom. This is why advertisers rely on a handful of Epicurean themes — happiness, youthfulness, success, status, luxury, fashion, beauty — to peddle their products. Their general implicit message is that solutions to human problems can be found in buying and consuming. You can join the *Pepsi Generation* to be a part of the action, wear a *Benetton* sweater to help unify the world, or save the environment by buying some recyclable garbage bag!

Leiss, Kline & Jhally (1990: 5) synthesize the various components (media, strategy, techniques, and themes) that have characterized the historical development of modern advertising (from 1890 to the present day) into a table, which I have modified slightly here to summarize the foregoing historical sketch and discussion:

Media	Print	Radio	Television	
Marketing Strategy	Rational	Non-rational	Behaviorist	Segmentation
Advertising Strategy	Utility	Product Symbols	Personification	Lifestyle
Period	1890-1920	1920-1950	1950-1970	1970-present
Focus of Advertising	product qualities, prise, use, etc.	product, qualities, symbolic attributes, etc.	product, person prototype	product, activity (person-setting)
Themes	quality, usefulness, etc.	status, family, health, social authority, etc.	glamour, romance, sensuality, self-transformation, etc.	leisure, health, groups, friendship, etc.

By *rational* vs. *non-rational*, Leiss, Kline & Jhally are referring to advertising texts designed to appeal to the reasoning mind *(rational)* versus those aimed at appealing to the emotions and at evoking hidden desires *(non-rational)*. The former type of advertising, which characterized the period from 1890 to the early twenties, focused on the utilitarian aspects of the product itself — its qualities, its price, its functions, etc.; the latter (which typified advertising during the twenties, thirties, forties, and part of the fifties) emphasized the symbolic attributes associated with a product — status, family, etc. The focus on personality models in advertisements coming out of the fifties, sixties, and part of the seventies — glamour, romance, sensuality, etc — is labeled aptly *behavioristic* by Leiss, Kline & Jhally; while the current emphasis on lifestyle (person and setting) is appropriately called *segmentation*, so as to highlight the technique employed by present-day advertisers of "segmenting" lifestyle symbols and behaviors, and then putting them together in various combinations and forms into magazine ad and TV commercial texts.

Advertising as a Social Text

At this point, it is important to debunk two widespread myths that the controversy and debate over advertising has generated in society at large. First of all, although there is now a substantial literature on all aspects of advertising, no consensus has yet been reached as to its efficacy in inducing the consumption of products. Advertising, in my view, is simply not as effective as many would claim it to be. Second, even though advertising is attacked by both "right-wing" groups for promoting secular humanism and sexuality and by "left-wing" ones for deceitfully influencing and promoting stereotypical role models, there is no solid evidence to establish that advertising has any formative effects on people. Advertisers do no more than to "speak to the already converted." By this I mean that advertisers aim their messages at specific groups and individuals who already possess (or aspire to possess) the lifestyle attributes and behaviors represented in their ad texts. They do this by means of two marketing strategies: *positioning* and *brand image*. *Positioning* is the placing or targeting of a product for the right people. For example, perfume ads of *Drakkar noir* are positioned for a male audience, whereas ads of *Chanel* are positioned, by and large, for a female audience. The marketing of *Audis* and *BMWs* is aimed at socially upscale car buyers, the marketing of *Dodge vans* is aimed, instead, at middle-class suburban dwellers. *Brand image* is the creation of a "personality" for the product. This implies that a product's name, packaging, price, and advertising textuality should create a recognizable personality for it that is meant to appeal to specific consumers. Take beer as an example. What kinds of people drink *Budweiser*? Your answer would probably include remarks about the educational level, class, social attitudes, etc. of the targeted consumer. The personality of the one who drinks *Budweiser* is vastly different from that of the one who drinks *Heineken*. The former is perceived to be a rough, vulgar, country-and-western type character; the latter a smooth, sophisticated, yuppie type. Note as well that *Budweiser* commercials are positioned next to sports events on television, whereas *Heineken* ads are found primarily in "high brow" magazines. The idea is to speak directly to the one who drinks a certain kind of brand, so that consumers can see their own personalities in terms of the lifestyle personalities with which the products they consume or buy are promoted.

In my opinion, rather than thinking of advertising as a subliminal form for persuasion, it is perhaps more appropriate to view it as a powerful *social text*. Textuality will be discussed more fully in the second chapter. Suffice it to say here that today most of our information, intellectual stimulation, entertainment, and lifestyle models come from, or are related to, media images and portrayals. We assimilate and react to advertising texts unwittingly, in ways that parallel how individuals and groups respond unconsciously to religious texts as templates for planning, interpreting, and structuring social actions and behaviors. Advertising has become one of the most ubiquitous, all-encompassing social texts ever devised by humans. As the great Canadian communications theorist Marshall McLuhan (e.g. 1962, 1964) pointed out several decades ago, the *medium* in this case has indeed become the *message*.

Whatever the behavioral effects of advertising — and there is no reason to believe that psychologists have any particular claim to knowing what these effects are! — from a semiotic standpoint what can be said, in my opinion, is that there are three kinds of *mediated effects* associated with lifestyle-based advertising whose manifestations are easily detectable in the population at large. I have referred to these elsewhere as the *mytholo-*

gizing effect, the *event fabrication effect*, and the *information compression effect* (Danesi 1994).

By *mythologizing effect* I am referring to the fact that advertising often imbues its characters with a mythological aura. The personages in many ads and commercials are intentionally sculpted to look like mythic heroes. Their "actions" in ads are thus often perceived to constitute events of momentous proportions, almost unreal and other-worldly happenings. Ad personages are infused with this deified quality not only by their "looks," but also by virtue of the fact that they are "seen" inside the mythical space created by the ad or commercial. By *event fabrication effect* I am referring to the common perceptual state that advertisements induce in their viewers. Ads and commercials transform some ordinary happening (a kiss, a glance, etc.) into a momentous *event*. This is because the *medium* in this case holds up —*encodes* — certain events as significant and meaningful. We perceive a glance from a beautiful model (male or female) in an ad or commercial as somehow worthy of emulation, a kiss as meaningful; and so on. By *information compression effect* I am referring to the fact that advertising presents information globally and instantly, inhibiting reflection on the topics, implications, words, etc. contained in a text. This has led to a new way in which we now tend to perceive messages and meanings. As a culture, we have developed short attention spans that require constant variety in information content. We have become habituated to large doses of visual images and catchy phrases edited and stylized for effortless mass consumption by advertisers.

Semiotics and Advertising

It was probably Roland Barthes (1957) who first drew the attention of semioticians to the value of studying the field of advertising. Barthes inspired the first semiotic works analyzing *signification*, or meaning-making, in ads. Today there is considerable interest in the semiotics of marketing (e.g. Umiker-Sebeok 1987, Umiker-Sebeok, Cossette & Bachand 1988; for a recent bibliography of work on the semiotics of marketing see Umiker-Sebeok 1989). If there is one theme that can be extracted from this line of inquiry which is of specific relevance to the present discussion, it is that many ads are interpretable at two levels — a "surface" level and an "underlying" one. The surface level contains the actual iconic and verbal signs of the ad. These are both the "reflexes" of, and the "traces" to, the underlying level: i.e. the surface elements cohere into a signifying system that conjures up an array of connotative meanings embedded in the underlying system. More often than not, these inhere in mythic, or archetypal, structures that work psychologically at a subthreshold level of mind. This is why ads for lifestyle products (perfume, clothing, etc.) often create genital and taboo ritualistic symbolism. Indeed, when the underlying *subtext* is decoded we tend to become alarmed and repulsed by the ad's so-called "hidden" message.

The science of *semiotics* grew out of the study by the ancient physicians of the Western world of the observable patterns of physiological symptoms induced by particular diseases in terms of how people experienced them. The first doctors apparently realized that the phenomenon of "disease" could only be understood in terms of a mind/body/culture relation.

The etymology of the term *semiotics* is traceable to the Greek word *sema* "marks, signs" (singular *semeion*). It is commonly defined as the science or "doctrine" (in the sense of systematic study) of signs. A *sign* is anything — a word, a gesture, an object, etc. — that stands for something or someone in some capacity. Therefore, anything in the world is eligible to become a sign. The color *green* becomes a sign the instant it is used to stand for the traffic command "go," for a verbal expression designating envy *(He's green with envy)*, and so on. Signs literally *represent* the world of beings, objects, ideas, and events: i.e. they "present them again" within the confines of mental space. They allow us, figuratively speaking, to carry the world around with us in our heads. Note as well that the "substances" used to make signs vary widely. A sign can be a physical object (e.g. a traffic sign), a word, a kind of sound (as in the Morse code), etc. Signs are the elements of such common *codes* as hand gestures, facial expressions, language, music, paintings, religious ceremonies, architectural styles, car designs, body image, sports events, clothing — in a nutshell, anything that has been *made* (invented, constructed, thought up, devised, etc.) by humans. Signs can be thought of as the "materials" we need and employ to create our artifacts, from words to social institutions. Human beings are indeed *makers*: they constantly make with their hands and with their minds. In fact, humans never stop making, at home, at work, and during leisure hours. There is something in our nature that seems to constantly drive us to make things.

The technical study of advertisements lends itself particularly well to the semiotic method. As Bell (1990: 1) has observed, the semiotic approach has not only been used by critics of advertising, aiming to bring to the surface the hidden meanings of advertising texts, but also by the advertisers and marketing managers themselves, who have found it to be a useful analytical tool in helping them determine how a commercial or ad text is working and, thus, in identifying weaknesses in the text. As Bell (1990: 1) puts it:

> Advertising is all about meaning. In marketing terminology, much advertising research has been concerned with the "message take out" from the commercial. In other words, what did the consumer understand from the commercial? What did it mean? More important than that...*how* it means.

Defining Semiotics

As mentioned above, in its oldest usage the term *semiotics* was coined by the ancient physicians. Hippocrates (460?-377? B.C.) — the founder of medicine — viewed the ways in which a disease was reported by patients as the basis upon which to carry out an appropriate diagnosis and upon which to formulate a suitable prognosis. By the time of Aristotle (384-322 B.C.), the term *semiotics* came to be used more generally for the study of all kinds of signs, not just bodily symptoms. In his *Course in General Linguistics* of 1916, compiled by his students after his death from the notes they took during his university course, the Swiss linguist Ferdinand De Saussure (1857-1913) used the term *semiology*, instead, to refer to the systematic study of signs. Saussure coined this term in obvious analogy to other terms ending in *-logy* (from Greek *logos* "word"). Saussure's term bears witness to his apparent belief in the supremacy of language as a representational code.

Nowadays, the term *semiotics* is preferred, given its generality. It is the term that will be used throughout this text. An interesting definition of *semiotics* is provided by Umberto Eco in his 1976 book, *A Theory of Semiotics.* Eco, incidentally, is the author of the best-selling novels *The Name of the Rose* and *Foucault's Pendulum,* which have stimulated a lot of interest in semiotics among the public at large. He defines semiotics as "the discipline studying everything which can be used in order to lie," because if "something cannot be used to tell a lie, conversely it cannot be used to tell the truth; it cannot, in fact, be used to tell at all" (Eco 1976: 7). This is, despite its apparent facetiousness, a rather insightful definition. It implies that we have the capacity to represent the world in any way we want through signs, even in misleading and deceitful ways. This capacity for subterfuge and artifice is a powerful one indeed.

The definition that has become the most widely adopted one is the one put forward by the American logician and mathematician Charles Sanders Peirce (1839-1914), who along with Saussure is considered to be the founder of the modern study of signs. He defined semiotics as the "doctrine" of *signs*, the latter being anything that "stands to somebody for something in some respect or capacity" (Peirce 1958/2: 228).

At first, Peirce's definition of *sign* might seem to be too vague and somewhat confusing. But consider again the example of the color *green*. Is it a sign according to Peirce's definition? Yes, because it is *something*, in this case a physical property of light, which *stands to somebody* (a motorist, a pedestrian, a speaker of English, etc.), *for something in some respect or capacity* ("go," "envy," etc.). So, while Peirce's definition might appear initially to be nebulous, it is actually a rather clear and concise one.

An Illustration of Semiotic Method

Consider, as a first case-in-point of how to decode advertisements semiotically, the *Russell & Bromley* shoe ad that was found in many "high class" magazines a few years ago (fig. 1). The first thing to keep in mind about any advertisement is that it is itself a *sign* — something that stands for something else. At the same time, there are many signs within the ad that cohere thematically to weave a message.

Saussure saw the *sign* as being made up of two parts: a *signifier* and a *signified*. The *signifier* is the physical part of the sign, the actual substance of which it is composed (sound-waves, alphabet characters, hand movements, visual forms, etc.); the *signified* is the object or mental concept to which it refers. The first signifiers to notice in the *Russell & Bromely* ad are the color tones. The young, attractive woman in the ad is dressed entirely

Fig. 1 — Ad for *Russell & Bromley* shoes

in white except for her shoes and for the color of her hair. Her leather pumps are partially dark blue and her hair is dark brown. The shoes and hair "stand out" because of the fact that the different color signifiers are in *paradigmatic opposition*. A sign enters into two fundamental relations with the other signs that form a specific *code*. It must, first, have some feature in its signifier that allows our perceptual system to differentiate it from all other signs. In the case of the contrasting white and dark colors of the ad, we are able to keep two areas of the girl's appearance (her shoes and her hair) distinct from other parts of the scene. This differentiation relation is known as *paradigmatic* structure. *Signification* cannot occur without such paradigmatic relations between signs.

As the sign enters into a paradigmatic (differential) relation with other signs in a code, it simultaneously forms combinatory and associative patterns with them. These are known as *syntagmatic* relations. The dark and white colors of the ad are both distinguishable and easily combined into a syntagmatic pattern: e.g. the white color of the dress is associated with several other features of the ad — the lace curtain, the walls and steps, the woman's purse, and the color of the lettering.

It should be noted that signs and their relations have *structure*, a discernible shape, pattern, or form that allows them to "fit" into a code. For example, the elements {*a, b, c, d, e*...} have a shape or form that assigns them to the code known as "the Roman alphabet." On the other hand, the elements {1, 2, 3, 4, 5...} reveal a structure that assigns them to a different code, known as "the integers." Signs can be thought of as pieces in a jigsaw puzzle. These have visual features on their "faces" that keep them distinct from each other, as well as differently-shaped "edges" that allow us to join them together in specific ways to complete the overall jigsaw picture. The word *structure* refers to the fact that signs relate to each other in specific and easily recognizable patterns, just like the pieces of a jigsaw puzzle.

Charles Peirce related the connection between sign and referent — signifier and signified — to the vagaries of the human interpreter. Peirce did not, however, view signification as *necessarily* open-ended; but rather that it was *potentially* infinite. For Peirce, we will always find some new meaning in some context for a sign, no matter how conventionalized the sign's utilization may have become. He called this aspect of the sign the *interpretant*. Peirce also provided us with a triadic typology of signs which has now become part of the standard lexicon of semiotic theory and practice. He differentiated among *icons, indexes* and *symbols* as the primary kinds of signs human beings use to represent the world. He did not, however, see these as mutually exclusive. Signs can, for instance, be partially iconic and symbolic: e.g. the cross in Christian religions stands both for the actual shape of the "cross" on which Christ was crucified (iconic sign) and "Christianity" (symbolic sign) *at the same time.*

An *icon* is a sign that resembles its referent in some way — e.g. "a pack shot in a commercial stands for the pack" (Bell 1990: 3). In Saussurean terms, it can be defined as a sign in which the signifier is made to look or sound like the signified. Photographs, maps, Roman numerals such as I, II, and III, etc. are all iconic signs because they are meant to portray their signified in some isomorphic — visually imitative — way. Onomatopoeic words such as *drip, bang, screech,* etc. are signifiers made to be intentionally sound-imitative of their referents. Iconicity, or mimetically-motivated representation, can be found in many of our cultural artifacts and works of art. Commercially-produced perfumes, for instance, can be designated as *artificial icons* of animal smells indicating sexual stimulation or arousal.

In the *Russell & Bromley* ad, there are several iconic cues that will ultimately lead to a plausible interpretation. Not only are the paradigmatically-related colors *dark* and *white* iconic signs, but note the configuration of the woman's legs and the vulvic shape of the folds made by her skirt. The vaginal "V-shape" can also be seen in the configuration of the woman's arms and legs.

An *index* is a sign with a direct existential connection to its referent. Smoke is an index of fire; a cough is an index of a cold; and so on. The most typical manifestation of indexicality is the pointing *index* finger. We use this to point out and locate beings and things in the environment. As such, indexicality is tied to a more fundamental force of semiosis that semioticians call *deixis,* which is defined simply as the process of locating objects, beings, and events in the world. Deixis can also involve the language code. Words such as *here, there, up, down,* etc. all imply spatial location. Indexicality and deixis probably reflect an inherent feature of cognition that can best be described as an extension of the sense of sight to track or locate beings, things, and actions into the domain of abstract thought. In the *Russell & Bromley* ad the dark toes of the shoes point indexically to the lettering of the ad. In this way, both the product name and the "direction" that the woman is seemingly about to take are highlighted suggestively.

A *symbol* is a sign that has an arbitrary or conventional relation to some referent. Words in general are symbolic signs. But any signifier — object, sound, figure, etc. — can take on symbolic significance. A cross can stand symbolically for the concept "Christianity;" a "V" configuration made with the index and middle fingers can stand symbolically for the concept "peace;" and so on. The use of the symbolic mode of interpretation is, in fact, the one that will ultimately allow us to decode the *Russell & Bromley* ad.

But before attempting an interpretation, it is important to make a clear-cut distinction, from the very outset, between *meaning* and *signification*. The former is used generally in semiotics in its broad dictionary definition of "anything that is intended," or "anything of some value to human beings." This constitutes an obvious logical circularity that cannot be avoided. In their 1923 work, titled appropriately *The Meaning of Meaning*, Ogden & Richards gave 23 meanings of the word *meaning*, showing how problematic a term it is. They also made a key distinction between *meaning* on the one side, and *sense* and *reference* on the other. For Ogden & Richards, what we call *sense* alludes etymologically to the physical nature of meaning. A sign must be received and perceived by our "biological sensors," so to speak, before it can have any "meaning" in the first place. At this basic level, meaning is anchored in a reaction to the content represented in the sign. *Reference*, on the other hand, is the process by which our sense reactions and thoughts are connected to reality through the use of signs: i.e. a sign *refers* (is connected to) some object, being, event, idea, etc. *Signification* is a much more specific term. It denotes, as its name implies, the thoughts that a sign evokes.

It is obvious that the use of signs to create messages and meanings entails an *interpretation*. This involves, in Peircean terms, knowing that something is in fact being used to stand for something else. Peirce designated the "something" used as the *representamen*, rather than *sign*, and the "something else" as the *object*, rather than the *referent*. He knew that problems in associating the *sign/representamen* to the *object/referent* were always bound to arise because the range of interpretation always varies from individual to individual. Peirce referred to this aspect of the sign as the *interpretant*. For Peirce, it is this "triangular relation" that coheres into the signification process. The reader should be aware, therefore, of the fact that all the "interpretations" put forward in this book are subject to my own subjective responses to each advertisement. The reader may or may not agree with my interpretive proposals, may see more into an advertisement along the suggested lines of interpretation, or may see nothing at all in it. This is a normal feature of *interpretation*. There is no *one* meaning to a human-made text. The purpose in this book is not to impose a specific interpretation on the reader, but to illustrate an analytical methodology.

The sign's primary meaning is called its *denotation*. This is the meaning or referential connection established between *signifier* and *signified*. But this meaning core can be extended freely to other domains of reference. This extensive process is known as *connotation*. Consider the word *house*. Its denotation can be paraphrased as "any structure for human habitation." The denotative uses of this sign can be seen in utterances such as "I bought a new *house* yesterday," "*House* prices are continually going up in this city," "We repainted our *house* the other day," and so on. But, by connotative extension, the same sign can be used to mean such things as a "legislative assembly" ("The *house* is in session at this moment"), "audience" ("The *house* roared with laughter"), etc. Note, however, that the basic elements of the sign's denotative meaning must be present in its extended uses for signification and communication to be successful. So, in the above sentences the denotative elements "structure," "human," and "habitation" are necessarily implicit: a legislative assembly and a theater audience do indeed imply "structures" of special kinds that "humans" can be said to "inhabit." Any connotative utilization of the word *house* is constrained by this "semantic structure;" i.e. the word-sign *house* can be applied to refer to anything that involves or implicates humans coming together for some specific reason.

There is another use of the term *connotation* that is of great importance to the decoding of advertisements. It can be called more precisely *cultural connotation* — a meaning of the sign that reaches into the "fund of knowledge" of a particular culture. Specific colors at certain times of the year, for instance, *connote* traditions, values, and belief systems. In our culture *white* is often symbolic of "cleanliness," "purity," "innocence," whereas *dark,* its paradigmatic counterpart, symbolizes "uncleanliness," "impurity," "corruption." In the remainder of this book, the word *connotation* will be employed with this meaning in mind.

In the *Russell & Bromley* ad, whiteness can now be seen to connote the woman's purity and sexual innocence, and darkness a foreboding and impending transgression of this state of being. Digging deeper into the connotative symbolism of the ad, we can now surmise that the paradigmatic contrast of the two colors, white and dark, suggests a struggle between innocence and sexual experience. In our cultural mythology, this symbolism is an ancient one indeed. Is the woman suggestive of the mythic figure Persephone ready to be abducted and raped by Hades, the god of the underworld? Is this ad text a modern reenactment of this ancient mythic text? The mythic component of advertising will be dealt with more extensively in subsequent chapters. Suffice it to say here that a semiotic analysis of advertisements must always look for any potential mythic connotation, a powerful component of the unconscious mind.

Let us look more closely at various other connotative suggestions present in the *Russell & Bromley* ad. Shoes indicate a journey. So, we can now ask ourselves: Where is the woman in the ad about to go? Her flowing, unrestrained hair suggests a willingness to experience sexual satisfaction. Is the downward pointing of her shoes suggestive of a journey to the "underworld," to the "dark regions" of sexual experience? Supporting this interpretive hypothesis are several iconic cues:

- her skirt is made of lace — a fabric connoting a sensual texture in our culture;

- the folds of the skirt make the shape of the vagina — a shape reinforced by the configuration of her arms;

- the texture of the lace dress, together with the "feel" implied by the leather shoes and handbag, are easily perceived as fetishistic;

- the young woman's state of sexual readiness seems also to be signaled by her open legs and exposed knees, which invite the viewer to gaze upon her sexuality — an obvious voyeuristic "turn-on" as the saying goes;

- her posture and facial expression are, in fact, highly suggestive of sexual readiness and desire.

The idea of a descent into the "underworld of sex" is also suggested by the fact that the woman is sitting on the top step of a staircase that is obviously "leading downward." And, as mentioned, her shoes point down — to a world full of sexual desire and satisfaction that wearing *Russell & Bromley* shoes purportedly opens up. The steps of the staircase are made of concrete and are "cracked," the suggestion being that the underworld is opening up to engulf the woman. Symbolically, the doorway can now be thought of as a *portal*, leading from one state (innocence) to another (sexuality). The woman has just crossed the threshold of the portal, ready to be engulfed by the passions to be experienced in the new realm. The lace-covered doorway and her lace dress are residues of her previous state. The woman is apparently suspended between the two states, as is the viewer. The tension that this causes — like the tension produced before sexual orgasm — is powerfully ambivalent, creating excitement. The underworld is attractive but dangerous — this is the mythic undertone that permeates the whole ad. Wearing *Russell & Bromley* shoes allows any young "girl" to mature into a "woman" via the sexual experiences that wearing these shoes can make realizable. The implicit sinfulness of buying and wearing the shoes is tantalizing indeed.

As this example shows, "decoding" an ad semiotically involves knowledge of the various kinds of signs and of the relations inherent among them. These cohere into a signifying system that is anchored in cultural connotation. The following chart can be used to summarize the basic "semiotic cues" detected in the *Russell & Bromley* ad text that led to the connotative interpretation proposed above:

Sign Type	Signifying Process	Examples from the ad
index	by causal or existential connection with the referent (the referent can be figured out)	the shoes pointing to the lettering and to the implied "underworld"
icon	by resemblance (the referent can be reseen, reheard, etc.)	the white and dark colours ("innocence" vs. "sexuality"), the V-shape of the hands, arms, and folds made by the dress ("vaginal" imagery), the portal ("passage-way to

		sinfulness"), the staircase and cracked steps (a staircase leading to an "underworld" that is about to open up to engulf the woman)
symbol	by convention (the relation to the referent must be learned in a cultural context)	the connotations of the white-dark contrasts, the mythic allusions to a journey, the doorway as a portal, the fetishistic quality of leather and lace, etc.

Semiotics offers, obviously, a method that can be easily applied to the deciphering of the messages that advertisers, and especially lifestyle advertisers, weave into their texts. It is based on interpreting the connotative meanings of signs and the culturally-circumscribed codes that they form. *Semiosis* is the term used to refer to the innate capacity of human beings to produce and understand signs of all kinds, from those belonging to simple physiological signaling systems to those which reveal a highly complex symbolic structure. The renowned semiotician, Thomas Sebeok of Indiana University, defines *semiosis* discerningly as "the capacity for containing, replicating and extracting messages, and of extracting their significance" (Sebeok 1985: 452).

The study of *semiosis* has revealed that the human organism is predisposed to transform physical states into representational ones. The philosopher Susanne Langer (1948) convincingly argued half a century ago that, at a primary level of mind, we apprehend the world through "feeling;" i.e. we "feel" that the world has a structure. She called this the *presentational* form of cognition. When we attempt to explain our feeling states vis-à-vis some event or representation (such as a work of art), we are forced to reorganize it in terms of language and its linear semiotic structures. She called this the *discursive* form of cognition. This is a *re*-presentational form of thinking that will never be able to cover the entire range of presentational effects produced by a meaningful stimulus or text.

The advertising text works at a presentational level first. We react to it in terms of feeling. It is when we attempt an explanation of the text that we enter into a discursive mode of interpretation, subject to the constraints of the particular language being used. But, then, this is inevitable in any interpretive venture: in literary criticism, musicology, art aesthetics, etc. *Hermeneutics*, or the art of interpretation, is invariably a discursive technique that can never be objective and absolute. Indeed, in my view, the interesting and significant aspect of hermeneutics is that it allows ample space for differences in the interpretation of any text, opening up a potentially fertile dialectic on the meaning of the text. The next three chapters are, in effect, my own "hermeneutic excursions" into the meanings found in lifestyle advertising texts. Hopefully, these will engage the reader in a dialectic with me or, at the very least, lead him/her to reflect on how such texts generate meaning.

2

DECODING
ADVERTISEMENTS

Introduction

A few years ago, an ad for a man's perfume named *Versus* filled the pages of lifestyle magazines (see fig. 2). At first look, the ad seems intent simply on spotlighting four rugged, handsome men who presumably wear *Versus* to smell as good as they look. At this surface level, the ad seems to be merely saying: "To smell attractively like these men, all you have to do is to put on *Versus*." But a *semiotic* analysis will reveal that the ad is imbued with many subtle, symbolic connotations that transform it, at an unconscious level, into a highly suggestive text.

To start off, let's consider both the name of the perfume and the shape of the bottle. The name starts with a "V" and the bottle displays a V-shaped intaglio in its center. Notice as well that each of the men in the ad wears a shirt or jacket whose open collar makes a V-shape. This no doubt is meant, at one level, to strengthen the syntagmatic association between the perfume's name, *Versus*, and its manufacturer, *Versace*. But *Versus* is a word that connotes "opposition," "violation," and the V-shape "indentation," "cleft" and "fissure." The implication of "opposition" and "cleft" is also suggested by the fact that the word *Versus* crosses the entire ad, implying a line of separation between the men in the ad and the viewers of the ad. So, what does the ad mean?

Decoding the Versus *Ad*

Let's attempt a guess, or more appropriately, a few guesses. The ad is clearly aimed at affluent, young males who can afford to buy an expensive bottle of perfume. The young men in the ad are prototypes of what young (mid-twenties) urban professional males aspire to look like during leisure hours — hours devoted presumably to mate selection and/or sexual fulfillment generally. During the day, the ad seems to be saying, he wears a suit; during recreational time he wears "V-neck" apparel and *Versus*. So, one possible interpretation of the ad's meaning is that *Versus*

Fig. 2 - *Ad for* Versus *perfume*

fits in nicely with the kind of leisure activities that such male types engage in. It is a perfume designed to help them cross over, symbolically, from the work world to the leisure world — worlds that are in opposition. Now, reasoning mythically, one can argue that the former world is suggestive of the realm of Apollo — the god of male beauty and of the fine arts — and the latter the realm of Dionysus — the god of wine, the irrational, the undisciplined, and the orgiastic. Is *Versus* the olfactory means by which a modern Apollo can enter the enticing and erotically appealing Dionysian realm?

This mythic interpretation is strengthened by the fact that the V-shape of the men's collars and of the bottle design "points downwards," i.e. down toward the Dionysian underworld of carnality and unending physical pleasure. *Versus* is, in this interpretational framework, a statement about the conflictual nature of humanity, constantly oscillating between Apollonian and Dionysian extremes.

The use of dark colors can also be tied to this interpretative line of reasoning. Darkness in our culture connotes fear, evil, the unknown. Children are perpetually afraid of the dark; we stay away from dark forests; we talk of "black masses;" we expect our evil personages in movies and in fictional lore to be dressed in black (just think of how fictional evil characters like Dracula, Darth Vader, and others are portrayed); we sense that forbidden, mysterious, happenings occur at night; etc. The dark tones of the bottle are also suggestive that something dark and dangerous, but nevertheless *desirous*, is about to happen.

Versus thus would seem to invite the male viewer to "cross over" (across the page) into the dark underworld where his base, primal urges can be released and satisfied. This world casts dark shadows on the men's faces — shadows that cover the eyes, the mirrors of the soul. In the underworld, there is no soul, no spirituality, just carnality and cupidity. The V-shape intaglio of *Versus* is indicative of an "opening" into this underworld, a crevice that opens up below a Dionysian world of lust and indulgence.

Note as well that one of the men in the ad wears a leather hat and another a leather motorcycle jacket, both of which are suggestive of membership in motorcycle gangs. Leather has a fetishistic quality which, as Sebeok (1991: 121) observes, "bridges the gap between touch and smell." Scenes and images of sadism and masochism in our culture are often accompanied by a personage wearing leather. Are these, perhaps, the forbidden sexual pleasures that *Versus* makes possible?

To complete the interpretive picture being drawn, consider, once again, the V-shape intaglio of the bottle, of the first letter of *Versus*, and of the men's necklines. The perfume is meant for men to wear. Now, ask yourself, what sexual objective would men have in wearing the perfume? What is the specific target of their desire? The vaginal shape of the bottle, of the letter "V," and of the neckline configurations appears to answer this question rather bluntly. But, at this point in the hermeneutic line of reasoning undertaken, another interpretive path opens up. One can ask, in fact, whether the object of the men's desire is just the "opposite" of the vagina, as the name *Versus* suggests at a semantic level? In other words, does the perfume allow the men to descend even further into deeply-hidden homosexual desires? The good looks of the men, with their darkened eyes looking directly into the camera, muscular bodies, and sensuously-protruding lips, leather apparel, together with the absence of women in the ad, is strongly suggestive of homosexuality.

Whether or not the two interpretations put forward here are appropriate, the point I wish to make is that both are seemingly *possible*. The way the ad is laid out and designed creates an entangled web of ambiguous sexual and macabre connotations-- *darkness of the night = sexuality = forbidden pleasures = hidden homosexual urges* = etc.

There is obviously much more to perfume than smell in advertising! The *Versus* ad illustrates rather strikingly how powerful visual texts are in making messages and how they encompass various levels of interpretation, each with its own hermeneutic path for the analyst to pursue. In a certain sense, this ad is a small "work of art," which has, however, the aesthetically-trivial purpose of enhancing sales of a product. The iconic features of the ad (the suggestive shape of the perfume bottle and of the men's necklines, the effective juxtaposition of the word *Versus* across the page, the dark shadows, etc.), the symbolic connotations that these evoke (e.g. the allusion of the name *Versus* to "oppositional" tendencies), all intertwine thematically to create a *subtext* with many signifying ramifications.

The term *subtext* is used here to mean any message which a given text connotes that is not immediately accessible to interpretation. A *subtext* is a text hidden, implied, or embedded within a text. In the case of the above ad, the subtext can be unraveled in the constellation of connotations derivable from the name and shape of the bottle, from the dark shadows cast upon the men's faces, from the name of the product, and so on. *Intertextuality* refers to the feature by which some texts allude to other culturally-defined or culturally-institutionalized texts. As Sorgem (1991: 5) indicates, intertextuality is the "co-presence of two or more texts." The dark background, for instance, recalls a mythic text — the descent into the Dionysian underworld.

As discussed in the previous chapter, the contemporary advertising industry originated as a marketing strategy at the threshold of the present century. Semiotically, it can be claimed that the premise which propels this industry today is that an ad's consumption-inducing effectiveness is proportional to its capacity to evoke suggestive subtexts and intertexts. Whether or not the psychological effectiveness of this supposition is demonstrable empirically is besides the point of the present discussion. The purpose of this chapter is to cast an opening glance at the subtextual and intertextual meaning domains which ads and commercials seem designed to educe.

Denotation and Connotation in Advertisements

It should be pointed out from the outset that not all advertisements are designed to work connotatively through subtexts and intertexts. Classified ads, for instance, are normally laid out simply to relay information about some product or service. It is perhaps more accurate to say, therefore, that the "connotative potential" of advertisement subtexts is at a maximum in ads and commercials which promote the use of products associated with some aspect of lifestyle (perfumes, clothes, cigarettes, alcohol, automobiles, etc.) and at a minimum in classified ads. Indeed, one can conceive of subtextual connotation as an interpretative *continuum*, starting from zero connotation (pure denotation, informational content) at one end and maximum connotation (open-ended, ambivalent, ambiguous, highly metaphorical subtexts) at the other. Classified ads, ads in trade manuals, and the like tend to fall in the sector of the continuum nearest to the denotative end-point, whereas lifestyle ads tend to fall in the sector that becomes progressively more connotative (fig. 3):

zero connotation (denotation)	classified ads, ads in trade manuals, etc.		ads for lifestile products (perfume, clothes, etc.)	maximum connotation
increasing →	*degrees* →	*cd* →	*connotation*	→
informational content	denotative		highly connotative	**mythical metaphorical content**

Fig. 3 — *The Connotative Continuum in Advertisements*

Textuality and Codes

The word *text*, as it is used in semiotic theory, means something very specific. It literally designates a "putting together" of signifiers to produce a message, consciously or unconsciously. The text can be either verbal or nonverbal. In order for the text to signify something, one must know the code to which the signifiers in the text belong. If one listens to a verbal language that one does not know, for example, all one hears are "disembodied signifiers"— sounds, intonations, etc. that one intuitively knows cohere into verbal texts that carry some intended meaning, but to which one has no access. The "embodiment" of the verbal signifiers occurs only when one comes to know the language code to which they belong (its phonetic system, its grammar, its lexicon, etc.). This applies as well to nonverbal texts, like clothing, bodily movements, gestures, and the like. Texts are *coded* reflexes of both individual and communal experiences. When these are understood, or "appreciated," they take on meaning or signification. Musical performances, stage plays, common discourse exchanges, dance styles, religious rites, ceremonies, etc. are the *coded* texts that we regularly make, as individuals or groups, both to make meaning of the world and to make meaning within it. The word *context*, as its name clearly implies, is literally the surrounding, or *"con-*taining" environment in which a text is encoded and decoded.

Many of the social actions and routines that we commonly perform can also be thought of as texts, or "scripts," as some cognitive scientists now prefer to designate them. Script theory, especially as developed by Roger Schank (e.g. 1984), refers essentially to the knowledge structures (signs and codes) deployed automatically in typical social situations. These equip us with the capacity to negotiate social actions successfully. The connection between social actions and textuality or scripting is implied in the following statement by Schank (1984: 125):

> When we read a story, we try to evaluate the reasoning processes of the main character. We try to determine why he does what he does and what he will do next. We examine what we would do in a similar situation, and we try to make the same connections that the main character seems to be making. We ask ourselves, *What is he trying to do? What's his plan? Why did he do what he just did?* Any understanding system has to be able to decipher the reasoning processes that actors in stories go through...Sometimes people achieve their goals by resorting to a script. When a script is unavailable, that is, when the situation is in some way novel, people are able to make up new plans.

The *texts* that humans constantly make — speeches, common discourses, poems, myths, novels, television programs, paintings, scientific theories, musical compositions, advertisements, etc. — are "windows" that open out onto the landscape of consciousness and cognition. Our messages and texts become meaningful, or signifying, only if they are constructed with the semiotic substances of *codes.* These are the systems that contain specific kinds of signs and the relations that inhere among them. Language, dress, gesture, etc. are examples of codes. The signs in the language code, for instance, are sounds, words, tones, etc.; the relations among these signs cohere into the grammar and lexicon of the language. The signs in the dress code are the items of clothing that we wear; the relations include the ways in which we combine the items of clothing for various occasions, how we use clothing to indicate professional or social status, and so on. Codes are directive and highly influential of behavior. The social codes involved in greeting, fashion, manners, rankings, etc. are all effective shapers of how we think of others and of ourselves.

As an example, consider the connotations involved in the "social code of the automobile." Outside of this social code, the automobile can be defined simply as a human artifact whose primary objective is to extend the human organism's locomotive capacity (walking, running, etc.) in mechanical ways. But, as a social code, it designates much more. As a test of your knowledge of this code, think of the social connotations involved in driving a *Mercedes Benz* vs. a *Volvo.* If I were to ask you what type of person drives each one, you would immediately be able to provide me with a "socially meaningful" answer. Perhaps, you would say that lawyers, executives, and other highly-paid professionals drive a *Mercedes*, while professors, clerks, accountants, and the like drive Volvos. The reason for this is that the car's social connotations (and therefore its price, design, etc.) are *coded*. This same type of coding extends to all areas of social interaction: e.g. the types and brand names of food, cigarettes, beer, etc. we consume give off coded messages of who we are, or, at least, aspire to be in our society. These codes are regularly implicated in lifestyle advertising.

To the notion of coding, Barthes (1977) added the concept of *anchorage*, or the notion that visual images in advertisements are polysemous (i.e. the have many meanings), which are *anchored* by viewers to specific socially-meaningful domains. Ad texts are constructed with signifiers that imply an endless chain of signifieds from which the viewer can choose some and ignore others: i.e. the text's signifieds are *anchored* to specific meaning domains by specific interpreters.

Now, let us return to the *Versus* ad (fig. 2. It is obvious that its subtextual meaning depends on socio-contextual factors around which the interpreter tends to anchor his/her interpretation. The various connotations of darkness, of the V-shape, of leather, etc. have meaning only in if anchored in a cultural context. The interpretations of the *Versus* ad proposed above would, thus, be impossible, or literally "meaningless," in cultures which did not ascribe the same connotative signification to darkness, V-shapes, and leather. In other words, the interpretation of a text's subtextual connotations is anchored in both the interpreter and in the specific culture in which the interpretation takes place. The components involved in the act of interpretation — the interpreter, the text, the context, the code, the culture, the product, etc. — are inextricably intertwined.

The Surface Text

In applying semiotics to interpreting advertisements, the first step is to get a firm grasp on the actual text itself. Methodologically, this can be done by simply specifying or cataloguing its features.

As an example, consider a television commercial for *Miller* beer that was shown regularly during Sunday afternoon

football games on American television a few years back. The first
thing the semiotician should do is to describe the commercial
literally or denotatively in his/her own words: i.e. a semiotic
analysis of advertising texts should start off by simply cataloguing, or "narrating," all the elements of the text. My own paraphrase of the *Miller* commercial now follows:

> As the commercial begins, we see a young man who is seated
> at a bar counter in a crowded, smoke-filled room, with a beer
> glass nearby. He is surrounded by a group of male compan-
> ions. They are chatting and confabulating in the normal way
> young men are purported to do in such situations. At the other
> end of the bar, a matched group of males has congregated
> around another young, handsome "leader of the pack." At a
> certain moment, an attractive female enters the bar scene. In-
> stantaneously, the "leaders" of both male cliques make their
> way towards her. To block the second leader from getting to
> her first, the first male clique cuts off his path to the female in a
> strategic manner, leaving the first leader to "get his prize." The
> whole "action" is described by a voice that is reminiscent of a
> football play-by-play announcer. Even the ways in which the
> first male clique carries out its "blocking plan" is described as
> if it were an action play in a football game. The commercial
> ends with the expression *Love is a game* appearing on the
> screen.

Given that the commercial was shown — i.e. positioned — during football game telecasts, and given the actions that took place
in the text, an interpretation can now be attempted. In a nutshell,
the actions of the two cliques would seem to constitute a simula-
tion of a football action play between two teams. "Winning" the
game in this case is "getting to" the female prize. In order to ac-
complish this, the first male leader, or "quarterback," needs the
support of his "team" to be effectual in carrying out the crucial
play, which of course he is. By successfully blocking the path of
the other team's quarterback to the girl, the first quarterback
wins the "game." He "scores" sexually, as the saying goes. Interpreting the commercial text in terms of a football game is reinforced by the play-by-play description of an announcer whose
voice and descriptive style are made to emulate those of a well-
known television football announcer, John Madden, as well as by
the concluding statement that appears on the screen: *Love is a
game.*

　　To recapitulate, the first step in "decoding" advertisements, therefore, is simply to list the signifiers and the contextual
cues of the surface text that will eventually give us access to the
subtextual code and its signifieds. A summary of the surface

textual signifiers of the *Versus* ad and of the *Miller* beer commercial follows:

	Signifiers	Contexts
Versus perfume	dark colour	-men's eyes -men's clothes -bottle colour -whole scene
	V-shape	-apparel necklines -bottle intaglio -first letter of perfume name
	leather	-one man's hat -one man's jacket
Miller beer commercial	male leader of a clique	drinking beer in a bar scene
	two male cliques	surrounding their respective leaders
	female	enters the game situation
	action play	cutting off the other clique's leader
	result	The first leader "gets" the female

The Subtext

The semiotic analysis of an ad or commercial constitutes an act of *decoding*, i.e. of unraveling the *code* that may lie below the surface text. *Decoding* refers essentially to the fact that there is a connotatively-based code in the advertisement that unfolds in subtextual and intertextual ways. The opposite of *decoding* is *encoding* which refers, of course, to the converse process of creating codes. There are three relevant questions you must ask yourself when decoding an advertisement. After the description of the surface text, these constitute the next three "steps" that decoding entails:

• *For whom is the ad intended?* Knowing the characteristics of the intended audience helps to constrain the connotative range of interpretation.

• *Can the iconic and verbal features be interpreted connotatively?* If so, then look for the appropriate codes that they tap into.

• *What metaphorical and/or intertextual structures make up the subtext?* Generally, there is a metaphorical notion embedded in the subtext

(*Love is a game*) that provides a conceptual framework within which to examine the connotative features of the code. Intertextual connotations are commonly mythic in nature.

As the analyses of the *Versus* ad or of the *Miller* beer commercial reveal, it is helpful to know who the primary target of the product's and advertisement's subtext is. It is not always the case that a product intended for the consumption of males is advertised with male fantasies and psychological urges in mind. An ad for men's perfume can, and often is, aimed at female consumers, so that they can be induced to buy the product for their lovers, and vice versa.

The iconic configuration of the ad's or commercial's visual signifiers normally implies an "action" or a "scenario." The scene in the *Versus* ad suggests a secluded, dark place opened up by the perfume bottle; the scene in the *Miller* commercial suggests a football action play sequence.

That the subtext of such lifestyle ads is generally structured metaphorically is now a well-documented fact in the field of marketing semiotics. In the case of the *Russell & Bromley* ad of the first chapter, the subtext is anchored in at least one metaphorical interpretation — *Sex is a hidden or forbidden desire*. But, as we saw, there were several other interpretative paths that could have been pursued. Indeed, the metaphorical open-endedness of the subtext gives the ad its psychological richness. The more literal an ad, the less effective it is at a psychological level. Note that what is emphasized in the subtext of the *Russell & Bromley* ad is not the actual act of a sexual experience, but the feelings that accompany it on the "steps" leading down towards the realm that makes it possible.

The *Russell & Bromley* ad associates sex metaphorically with clothing. This is, in general, how we perceive the stylized wearing of clothes in our culture. At a fundamental, "biological survival" level, clothes have a very useful function indeed — they enhance our survivability considerably. They are, at this level, human-made "extensions" of the body's protective resources designed to counteract environmental fluctuations. They are artifactual, protective "additions," so to speak, to our bodily hair and skin thickness. At this primary level, *clothes* constitute universal, trans-cultural artifacts that have a unitary meaning-- they improve the ability of human beings to survive. As Werner Enninger (1992: 215) aptly points out, this is why clothing quality and styles vary according to geography and topography: "The distribution of types of clothing in relation to different climatic zones and the variation in clothes worn with changes in weather conditions show their practical, protective function." It is only when clothes are transformed into *dress* codes (from Old French *dresser* "to arrange, set up") that they take on culture-specific connotations. In the artifactual realm of culture, therefore, clothes become signifiers that are associated, by connotation and various metaphorical and metonymic processes, with a whole range of signifieds. This "transformational" model of cultural signification applies to any object, substance, etc. that is mapped from the biological level to the cultural-symbolic one via signifying processes:

Cultural World
↑
The object, item, substance, etc. takes on signifying power
↑
Clothes are transformed into dress codes with connotative meanings
↑

Signifying Process
↑
Connotation,
metaphor,
metonymy, etc.
↑
These convert the world
of objects into signifying codes
↑

Biological World
↑
Objects, items, substances, etc., are adapted to enhence survivability
↑
These are "extenders" of bodily functions
↑
Clothes extend the body's environmental protective system
↑
The body has an environmental protective system (bodily hairs, thick skin, etc.)

Fig. 4- *A Transformational Model of Cultural Semiosis*

The making of clothes at the biological level enhances survivability. We would hardly be able to get through a Canadian winter, for instance, without appropriate clothing. When this human-made fabric--*cloth*--is transformed by some signifying process (connotation, metaphor, metonymy, etc.) within a specific cultural context, a new constellation of meanings is assigned to it. The particular characteristics of this new code, or meaning system, will differ among persons and among cultures. Although it evolved out of the biological level, in the world of culture clothing is subject to much variation and interpretation. Indeed, going back to Eco's definition of semiosis as the capacity to lie and deceive (chapter 1), we can even use clothing to lie: con artists and criminals can dress in three-piece suits to look trustworthy; anyone can dress like a policeman, whether or not he/she is an officer of the law in reality; and so on. To avoid the possibility of deceiving via clothes, some societies have even enacted laws that strictly define dress codes. In Ancient Rome, for instance, only aristocrats were allowed to wear purple-colored clothes; in medieval Europe peasants were required to wear their hair short, because long hair was the privilege of the aristocracy; in many religiously-oriented cultures, differentiated dress codes for males and females are regularly enforced; and the list could go on and on.

The association between clothing and sexuality is an ancient one. As Helen Fisher (1992: 253-254) aptly observes, even in the jungle of Amazonia Yanomamo men and women wear clothes for sexual modesty. A Yanomamo woman would feel as much discomfort and agony at removing her vaginal string belt as would a North American woman if one were to ask her to remove her underwear. Similarly, a Yanomamo man would feel just as much embarrassment at his penis accidentally falling out of its encasement, as would a North American male caught literally "with his pants down." We are, in fact, the only animal that does not "go nude," so to speak, without triggering off some form of social repercussion (unless, of course, the social ambiance is that of a so-called "nudist camp"). Indeed, *nudity* can only be defined culturally. We are all born *nude*, but we soon learn that this bodily state has special connotations during our childhood years. Moreover, what is considered "exposable" of the body will vary significantly from culture to culture, even though the covering of genitalia seems, for the most part, to cross cultural boundaries.

Subtexts create symbolic associations between the product and what consumers covet (brand image). Take, for example,
Budweiser vs. *Heineken* beer. To my own flavor buds, both beers
taste about the same. So, the "difference" between the two beers
is to be sought at a different level. Simply put, *Budweiser* ads
speak to a working class audience, while *Heineken* ones speak to
an socially upscale one. This is why *Bud* ads and TV commercials
are set in working-class bars which play hard rock or country
and western music, where people wear cowboy-style clothes and
boots, where the men look rugged and tough, and where the
women appear to be very little more than sex objects. The subtext in these ads is: "You're one of the guys, bud," so "this *Bud's*
for you!" *Heineken* ads, on the other hand, show a much more
sophisticated scene — nightclubs, country clubs, fashionable
restaurants — where yuppie customers seemingly listen to soft
rock, jazz, or even classical music, where the men look country-
clubbish, suave, and debonair, and where the women are chic,
sophisticated, charming.

Myths and Mythologies in Advertisements

Sexuality is also ensconced in mythic themes and narratives that
undergird the subtext. This is why the *Russell & Bromley* ad can
be decoded in terms of the Persephone myth. The feeling of
mystery and fear that sexuality engenders constitutes the source
of many archetypal or mythic structures in the unconscious
mind. The image of the "huntress," for instance, can be seen to
have sexual-erotic mythic connotations in most Western societies. This is perhaps why the image of a fierce, powerful, and
sexually dangerous female surfaces in all kinds of popular narratives — from ancient myths such as that of Diana to contemporary movies such as *Fatal Attraction* and *Basic Instinct*. The figure
of the "female-as-huntress" seems to form a kind of paradigmatic cultural counterpart to the figure of the "female-as-
mother."

The word *myth* derives from the Greek *mythos* "word,"
"speech," "tale of the gods." It can be defined as a metaphorical
narrative that seeks to give order and coherence to experiences
and perceived events by relating them to some existential purpose in terms of time (sequentiality), space (location, eventual-
ity), and cause (ascribed to some metaphysical entity, happening,

or event). In the primordial stages of human culture, myths were genuine "theories" of the world, aiming to explain it with what the great Italian philosopher Giambattista Vico (1688-1744) called the *poetic imagination*. Mythical narratives continue to form the basis for imparting knowledge of the world to children *poetically* and *imaginatively*. There are no cultures without stories, fables, and legends to explain the origins of things, people, morals, values, etc.: the Zuni Indians, for instance, claim to have emerged from a mystical hole in the earth, thus establishing their kinship with the land; Rome was said to be founded by Romulus and Remus, two wolves; and the list goes on and on. Myth-creation and story-telling in general reveal something rather unique about humans. Unlike other animals, humans possess the demonstrable capacity to invent stories of all kinds, true or not. Narrativity appears to be a fundamental sense-making operation of the mind, and would seem to be universal throughout humanity (see, for example, Perron & Danesi 1993). It is a common experience that we remember stories more easily and vividly than we do isolated concepts and words.

The narrative structure of the myths of early cultures allows us to reconstruct the *forma mentis* of that people. The crucial thing to note is that the first myths have not disappeared. As psychoanalysis has maintained for years, there seems to be a kind of "mythic unconscious" in humanity embedded in a mental substratum shaped by our first stories. The "unconscious" mind, in turn, would seem to be a powerful shaper of conscious activity. This is, after all, the reason behind the use of so-called "subliminal" techniques in advertising. Whether or not the suasive effectiveness of such methods has ever been demonstrated is beside the point of the present discussion. The fact is that ad creators continually attempt to tap into powerful "mythic" themes and motifs in the unconscious mind.

According to some scholars of mythology (e.g. Campbell 1969, Heinberg 1989) our primordial acts of conscious social activity (hunting, gathering, etc.) constitute the source of many mythic themes. As Campbell (1969, 59-60) has observed, these encode fear and awe of the world of nature itself. The paleographical and archaeological record suggests rather unambiguously that human societies have progressed through a series of stages. During the primitive stages of all societies there is evidence that myth is the primary mode by which cultures come to establish communal sense-making. Not possessing the knowledge to understand or "explain" environmental events logically and rationally, the first humans ascribed them to awesome and frightful "gods" or "divine" creatures, thus producing humanity's first myths, stories, and archetypes (literally, an original model of something). In a succeeding stage of cultural evolution, societies then tend to look towards their own "human contexts" for the symbolic means to explain phenomena in the world. Out of these emerged the first *represented* "human dramas" with the "heroes" of the evolving culture as the major players in these dramas. Cognition was structured primarily by the mimetic mode of thinking and acting, but the overlapping narrative mode transformed these dramas into legends and history. At this secondary stage of cultural development, contextuality, the capacity to locate deep-level thought patterns into a historical context began to play a crucial role in the formation of a rational cognition and civilization. It was only at an advanced stage of cultural evolution, however, that rationality, or *discursiveness*, to use Langer's (1948) term again, became the dominant mode of cognition and social action.

Giambattista Vico was among the first to search for the origins of a specific culture on the proposition that the first thoughts of that culture could be reconstructed from the concrete meanings of the words, symbols, and myths used to express them (see Bergin & Fisch 1984). Myths were created to allow the first hominids living in groups to make sense of the world together, and their narrative structure can be seen to betray the actual metaphorical structure of human cognition. There is no irony, for example, in early myths and cultures. For Vico, irony is the characteristic feature of a highly abstract rationalistic state of mind. Irony is one of the four tropes that he identifies as fundamental to human language — metaphor, metonymy, synecdoche, and irony — and that it is the one that develops later, both phylogenetically and ontogenetically. Irony unfolds only in an advanced cultural context: i.e. it is a surface-level cognitive feature that emerges at the level of culture, not of primordial thought.

According to Roland Barthes (1957), advertising taps into the mythic level of mind, and into its contemporary crystallizations, which he labels *mythologies*. Mythologies are anchored in mythic connotation. In early Hollywood westerns, for instance, the mythic "good" vs. "evil" dichotomy was portrayed by having heroes wear white and villains black. Sports events are mythological dramas juxtaposing the "good" (the home hero or team) vs. the "bad" (the outsider or visiting team). The whole fanfare associated with preparing for the "big event," like the World Series of baseball or the Superbowl of American football, has a ritualistic quality similar to the pomp and circumstance that ancient armies engaged in before going out to battle and war. Indeed, the whole sports event is perceived to be a mythic battle. The symbolism of the "home" team's (army's) uniform, the "valor" and "strength" of star players (the heroic warriors), and the capacity of the coach (the army general) all have a profound emotional effect on the fans (one of the two warring nations). The game (the battle) is perceived to unfold in moral terms: it is a struggle of "righteousness" and "beauty" against the forces of "ugliness" and "baseness." Sports figures are exalted as heroes or condemned as villains. Victory is interpreted in moral terms as a struggle of good vs. evil. The game is, as the television and radio ads constantly blurt out, *Real life, real drama!*

Mythologies have great connotative power in all cultures. Without them, cultures would hardly be "human," restricted to carrying out only survival functions at a biological level. Sports events replace great battles, spectacles re-enact our need for ritual and dramatic performance, sweet sixteen birthday parties signal a "rite of passage," and the list could go on and on. The human-made world of culture is a mythological one.

This is why the presence of mythic themes and dichotomies in advertisements cannot but have an effect on us unconsciously. Myths allow us to define ourselves as individuals and as groups. Advertisements are, in a certain sense, texts that satisfy the need for myth in highly rationalized cultural contexts: i.e. while modern cultures no longer rely on myths to explain the world, they cannot replace the psychological power of the *poetic imagination*, which continues to thrive in different forms — in cultural mythologies, in superstitions, and in the connotative substance of many advertisements.

An Illustrative Summary

As an illustrative summary of how to go about the task of decoding an advertisement, let us take one other example. Recall that the overall line of attack inheres in a procedure that can be encapsulated by the formula: *from-the-surface-text-to-the-subtext*.

Consider the ad for *Iron Cologne* found a short while ago
in mainstream fashion magazines like *Cosmopolitan*, suggesting a
female viewing audience (fig. 5). The first step is to describe the
surface text. Here, we see a handsome, muscular, sensuous man
embracing a voluptuous woman dressed up for physical exer-
cise. The shade of the ad is bluish, the color of the cologne bottle.
At the bottom of the page is an insert showing the bottle of perfume being sprayed. The insert seems to be "underneath" the
main visual text: i.e. the actual ad text has been "ripped" at its
bottom right corner to expose the "hidden" cologne bottle. The
expression *Pump some iron*, completes the textual presentation.

At a denotative level, the message seems quite simply to
be: "Enjoy a great sex life, as physically energetic and satisfying
as pumping iron, by wearing *Iron Cologne*, or buying it for your
male partner." The message is apparently directed to both males
and females. "Denotative meaning," writes Hoshino (1987: 46),
"involves a product's surface meaning, which mainly implies its
technological and functional meaning (practical and substantial
meaning) and corresponds to the consumer's physical needs."

Let us now delve a little deeper into the connotative domains suggested by the text's signifiers. It is at this connotative
level where, as Hoshino (1987: 46) also observes, "a product's
deep and hidden meaning, which tacitly and vaguely suggests a
non-material meaning...corresponds to the consumer's psychological needs." First, the blue shading is not only synchronized
with the color of the cologne bottle, but it could also suggest the
"shadow of nighttime," an appropriate time during which to
enjoy sex. A closer look at the implied action in the ad reveals
that the male is holding the female's hair forcibly, coercively,
violently. He is looking down at her. Her eyes, on the other
hand, are shut, passively, submissively. Note as well that we do
not see where his other hand is (Could it be fondling her?). It
would appear, in short, that the man is about to force the woman
down into a supine position for sexual intercourse.

Note, as well, the paradigmatic juxtaposition of shading
in the ad: she is dressed in white; he is dressed in black. This is
connotative, as mentioned above, of a "good vs. evil,"
"innocence vs. sexuality" dichotomy. The implicit violence of his
embrace is reinforced by the ripped insert at the bottom of the
page. The act of ripping is forceful and passionate. This is why
we commonly say such things as *He ripped off her clothes*. Also,
the exposure of the spraying bottle perhaps reveals what is

Fig. 5 - Ad for *Iron Cologne*

"underneath" the male's violent act of passion. His desire, in masturbatory or intercourse terms, is indeed that of a "spray" (ejaculation). The bottle is being sprayed, as a matter of fact, in the same direction as the male's orientation. The finger on the sprayer is an indexical sign, pointing out the bottle, the source of his sexual satisfaction.

This subtextual analysis is highly synchronized with our culture's view of masculine sex as violent and that of female sex as passive and receptive. The female in the ad seems to be quietly and passively enjoying his act of coercion.

At this point, the verbal component of the text, *Pump some iron*, can be easily connected to the subtext. At the surface textual level, it can be related to the physically-invigorating act ensuing from intercourse. But in terms of the hypothesized subtext it suggests the nature of male sexuality as it is perceived in our culture: one must "pump" the "head" of the bottle (in the same way that one masturbates). *Pumping iron* also describes a body-building activity, which is also in line with the perception of male sexuality as strong, violent, and dominant. The man's muscular arms reinforce this interpretation. Finally, it is not uncommon to refer to the sex act colloquially as "pumping," with the "iron" being an obvious metaphor for an erect penis.

The iconic configuration of the three words, *Pump some iron*, is also connotatively-suggestive. The three words are presented "one on top of the other," which is indicative of the normal supine position for sexual intercourse. And the sounds of the words themselves, when uttered out loud, suggest the kind of grunting that accompanies sexual intercourse.

This analysis of the subtext of this ad makes sense only in a cultural context where masculine sexuality is perceived as aggressive and dominating and female sexuality as passive and submissive. Since the ad appeared in women's magazines, it is highly likely that the message to the female viewer is: "In order to be attractive to your aggressive partner, you must be perceived to be passive and submissive to his 'iron'." Violent sex, which is pleasurable presumably to men, is filtered for the female viewer through the blue shading and soft glare of the ad's color.

To conclude, the analytical approach discussed in this chapter is the normal one followed in decoding advertisements. I wish to emphasize once again, that the interpretations put forward by a particular analyst are only *that--possible* interpretations. Interpretations exist on a "connotative continuum," as suggested above; they should always be compared, discussed, and tested further against other ad texts for the same product, since the codes and themes associated with a product are often repeated in different guises and forms. The following chart synthesizes the hermeneutic technique involved in decoding advertisements:

Decoding Level	
Surface Text	**Subtext**
denotative description of the text's signifiers and implied actions	culture-specific analysis of the connotations associated with the signifiers and actions: What do the signifiers connote vis-à-vis the uses of the product? Does the ad recall any mythic intertext? Is there a metaphorical structure implied

Before closing this chapter, I wish to add a philosophical reflection. As the reader may have noticed in the foregoing analyses of advertisements, there appears to be an implicit aspect to advertising that cannot be underestimated — the emphasis on ego. As one decodes more and more ads, in fact, one eventually comes to the realization that advertisers perceive our culture to be an egomaniacal one. Almost without exception, ads speak to the ego. Diane Barthel (1988: 18) puts it appropriately as follows:

> Would-be advertising men are advised that the one word consumers never tire of is *me*. Advertisers simply tell them who that "me" is, and how to make it ever more attractive, comfortable, exciting, appealing. To do this, advertisers must do more than communicate information on a product. They must communicate *image*. Their task is somehow to position a product within a market of competing goods and to aim it toward an identifiable population. They must give it a personality.

ICONIC FEATURES

Introduction

As illustrated in the previous chapter, a major component of decoding an advertisement's subtext consists in putting together it's visual elements into a coherent *iconic* text, i.e. into a narrative format that is implied or suggested by the visual features of the ad text. The purpose of this chapter is to go into more detail into the iconic features of advertisements. I will start off with a general discussion of iconicity. Then, I will deal with the iconic characteristics of advertisements. Finally, I will extract from the discussion and the various analyses some general methodological principles for decoding advertisements and commercials iconically.

Iconicity

For many semioticians, especially those of the Peircean school of thought, *iconicity* constitutes the primary mode of representation. The claim is that semiosis is at first tied to the operations of our sensory apparatus. It is only through repeated usage in cultural contexts that it eventually becomes free of sensory control. Iconicity, for many, lies at the core of how the human organism responds first and foremost to the world in its innate tendency to represent it.

Iconic signs, as discussed in the first chapter, are models of the world based on a perceived resemblance. The word *icon* derives, in fact, from the Greek word *eikon* "image." There exists evidence scattered all over the literature in the various human sciences to suggest that iconicity is indeed a fundamental modeling tendency in the human organism. As an example, consider the recent work of David McNeill (1992), who has done extensive cross-cultural research on the tendency to use gesture concomitantly during narrative discourse. His work has shown rather conspicuously how iconic thinking has power over the ways we conceptualize. McNeill argues that there is a unity between language and gesture. He has painstakingly analyzed, over a ten-year period, how individuals engaged in narrative discourse — of different cultures, children as well as adults, some even neurologically impaired — invariably manifest the tendency to represent the mental images inherent in discourse in terms of gestural forms. McNeill has shown, consequently, that gestures derive from a more fundamental, emotional, *presentational* level that has a visible impact on the ways in which narrative discourse is expressed. So, for instance, McNeill has shown that if one were to talk of "large" things, then one's hands would tend to show "largeness" by a cupping action that involves moving the hands outward in a kind of "swelling" motion. Vice versa, if the underlying focus of one's message was "smallness," then one would tend to use the opposite gesture. It seems, if McNeill is right, that we have a constant need to literally "draw" our thoughts with our hands.

Pictorial representation is an ancient, universal, abstract form of iconic expression. The research on children's drawings (e.g. Krampen 1991, Cox 1992) shows that children start representing their environment iconically at about the same time that they utter their first words. If a drawing instrument is put into the child's hand, that child will almost instinctively use it to draw — a "skill" that no one has imparted or transmitted to the child. This instinctual propensity to draw is manifest as well in doodling, which is probably a residual tendency of our childhood predilection to represent the world in visual images. All the artifacts discovered from the pre-civilized world bear witness to this "innate" modeling capacity in the human being. The child must be exposed to language in order for him/her to acquire it; that same child does not, however, need to be exposed to visual art in order for him or her to draw. If given drawing materials around the age of two or three, young children happily scribble randomly on the drawing surface. As time passes, however, their scribbling becomes more and more controlled; geometrical shapes such as crude circles, crosses, and rectangles, at first accidentally produced, are repeated and gradually perfected. Although children, with parental prompting, may learn to label circles as "suns" or "faces," they do not set out to draw anything in the environment, but instead seem spontaneously to produce forms that become refined through practice into precise, repeatable shapes. The act of making shapes is pleasurable in itself and appears to be intrinsically satisfying; usually identification is provided, if at all, only after the child finishes drawing. Of course, shapes eventually suggest "things" to the child as the ability to use symbols develops; but in the beginning, pleasure and satisfaction seem to occur without larger or more explicit associations of meaning. This form of activity in the presymbolic child is perhaps truly an example of "art for art's sake." Iconicity is clearly a fundamental force in symbol creation.

Iconicity is not limited to the visual channel. Audio-oral iconicity (onomatopoeia, imitative grunts, etc.) is a dominant force in semiosis as well. Children invariably emit sounds osmotically when they play to accompany their rhythmic movements, to imitate the sounds of their toys, and to generate emotional responses in other children. Speech itself evokes physiological responses because it literally issues forth from the body. The first words of children are, in fact, the result of osmosis intersecting with conceptual development.

In an ad text, we understand the iconic cues unconsciously as part of a system of meaningful representation because they are derived from of our codes of signification. In advertisements, iconicity usually takes the form of visual cues, although in commercials, musical and verbal components of the text can also be iconic. Television and radio commercials based on jingles, for instance, are grounded on the iconic principle that representation is more effective if it can be associated with some rhythm schema, or with some catchy, memorable tune. This is why a few years back, *Coca Cola* and*Pepsi* created commercials based on songs that could be easily remembered and hummed.

Visual Thinking

Visual or imagistic thought would seem to be a more fundamental form of cognition than is verbal, propositional thought. This is, actually, an implicit theme that can be extrapolated from a large portion of the research in developmental psychology. The Russian psychologist L. S. Vygotsky (1962), for instance, documented an "inner speech" stage in early childhood that is highly suggestive of an imagistic form of consciousness. This stage is characterized by the invention and use of words which are concrete models of referents. It is only after the child has acquired the particular grammar of his/her language that "verbal thought" would seem to overlap with this more fundamental mode of thinking, becoming indistinguishable from it. From that point onwards syntactic language gradually takes over as our primary bearer of thoughts. The conversion of experience into images is called "visual thinking" by the psychologist and art critic Rudolf Arnheim (1969), in order to differentiate it from conceptual, or verbal, thinking. Arnheim's main presupposition is that visual thinking, in the form of mental imagery, is the primordial, or "default" mode of cognizing. When we lack the appropriate language symbolism to represent some feeling, notion, or intuition, we literally "fall back" (by default) on our capacity to form mental images to help us out.

Mental imagery is not only "pictorial." It can also be musical and even verbal. One can literally "imagine" melodies and words as easily as visualizable scenes. Note how easy it is to visualize such familiar sensations, sounds, etc. as the laugh of a close friend, the sound of a baby crying, the feel of wet grass, the feel of a runny nose, the smell of fish, the taste of toothpaste, the sensation of being uncomfortably cold, the sensation of extreme happiness. A mental image, obviously, is an inner version of some sense impression or affective state. It can be a sound, a shape of an object, a smell, etc. Imagery would seem to share many of the same neural processes as the sensory perception system. This might explain why our vocabularies for visual sensation and mental perception share many elements. In actual practice, we rarely make a distinction between the two: sentences such as *I see the book on the table* (which implicates visual perception) are used in parallel with sentences such as *I see the point of your argument* (which implicates some abstract notion).

The topic of imagery has a long history in psychology and is ensconced in controversy. Individual differences in the ability to experience imagery were recorded first in the previous century. Throughout this century, the research that shows how mental imagery can be elicited is actually rather straightforward and, in my view, unambiguous. People can recall faces and recognize voices accurately and quickly, rotate objects in their heads, locate imaginary places in terms of so-called "cognitive maps," and scan specific scenic formats (game boards, room layouts, city streets, etc.) in their minds with no difficulty whatsoever. While researchers might disagree on exactly *what* it is that their subjects *see*, or *experience*, in their minds, they concur that something is "going on" in the mind. The American psychologist Stephen Kosslyn (e.g. 1983) and his co-researchers have been investigating how the brain's imagery system might work. In a series of ingenious experiments, Kosslyn has demonstrated how subjects can conjure up images of the arrangement of furniture in a room, of how to move a couch, of how to redesign a blueprint, etc. He has shown, in essence, how people construct elaborate mental images, search them out for specific purposes, and perform all kinds of visually-describable movements in their minds.

It is amazing to contemplate how a visual signifier, which cannot be felt by our sense of touch, can actually evoke a tactile sensation nonetheless. This is, in my view, strongly suggestive evidence that the senses are *intermodal*: i.e. that they mesh in the act of perception and sign interpretation. The term that best expresses the intermodality of sensation and interpretation is *synesthesia*--the sensation produced at a point other than, or remote from, the point of stimulation. When a visual figure evokes a tactile reaction, or when a sound evokes a visual signifier (color), the sensation is said to be synesthetic. Synesthesia refers as well to the juxtaposition of different sense modalities in semiosis. This is why we say that something is a *loud* color or a *bright* sound. The ability to evoke, and even replace, one sense modality by another explains why vision-impaired individuals can "see" objects by "touching" them. The term *aesthesia*, on the other hand, is commonly used to refer to the ability to experience sensation. When we call the appreciation of art an "aesthetic experience," we literally mean that we sense and feel the meaning of a work of art (presentational interpretation), even though it has been constructed through some conventionalized code (musical forms, painting styles, etc.).

Clearly, then, in analyzing an ad or commercial semiotically, the first step in getting to its subtextual level is to describe and decipher its visual-iconic presentational form. Recall, for example, the feel associated with lace and leather that was elicited synesthetically in the *Versus* and *Russell & Bromely* ads. This was crucial step in opening up the path to the subtext.

Analyzing the Advertisement Text Iconically

Consider, as a case-in-point of iconic analysis, the *Coco* perfume ad found recently in many magazines.[1] *Coco: l'esprit de Chanel* is an expensive women's perfume. The initial analytical step on the path leading to the subtext consists in describing the iconic features of its surface text. The first thing to note is a voluptuous, young woman dressed up to resemble a bird. She has a "tail;" she is tied down by a rope around her ankle; she is seated at the top of a staircase. The background is pitch dark, making both her and the oversized bottle of the perfume she is holding up stand out distinctly. She is clad scantily in sexy fishnet pantyhose and long black gloves. She is looking straight into the viewer's eye.

Now, we can begin our probe of the subtextual connotations that this visual scene elicits. Incidentally, the iconic features in this ad are not solely visual. The word *Coco* itself reinforces the bird signifier since it is clearly imitative of the word *cuckoo*. As a matter of fact, the semantic connotations of this word open up an indirect route to the subtext. It is a slang word for "crazy, wild, unconventional, uninhibited." Being *cuckoo* can also mean being "infatuated" and "obsessed." Furthermore, *Coco* is an abbreviation for *cocaine*, not only a narcotic, but also an aphrodisiacal intoxicant.

These iconic features raise the following questions:

•Who is the woman?
•Why is she dressed up as a bird?
•Why does she have a rope around her ankle?
•Who or what is holding the rope?
•Why is it so dark?
•Why is she dressed in this way?

Perfume is designed to be a sexual stimulant, a means for enhancing sexual attractiveness through the olfactory channel. At a surface level, the ad must be related to the product's function. And, indeed, the woman in the ad appears to be sexually desirable. Like a female bird sending out olfactory mating signals, we can almost smell her sexual scent synesthetically. Her

---

1. Chanel did not give permission to reproduce the ad. We beg the reader's indulgence.

bodily schema is indicative of voyeuristic poise. She is seemingly ready and approachable by the male of the species.

The darkness of the ad, as discussed throughout this book, is normally symbolic of the night, when sex and seduction take place. Darkness also connotes evil, mystery, danger, fear, and excitement. Black is the paradigmatic opposite of white, which symbolizes daylight, innocence, purity, safety, assurance.

A woman dressed in black signals sexual interest, sophistication, irresistible allure. But, like the black widow spider, a woman in black is not to be trusted.The representation of the human female as a bird is a deeply-embedded image in our culture. In English slang, for example, a young, pretty girl is called a *chick;* and the expressions *stuffing a bird* and *getting tail* mean "to have sex with a woman." The woman in the ad has black feathers, suggesting a syntagmatic chain of nefarious connotations. Black birds are associated with voraciousness, carnivorousness, insatiability. The woman, by implication, is perceived to be ravenous for sexual mating, with the same kinds of sexual instincts of a bird of prey.

But the ad is suggestive of many more meanings. Its connotative potential is at a maximum, given its ambiguity and ambivalence. In fact, the whole iconic scenario can elicit various syntagmatic chains of meanings. One is the *woman-as-pet* metaphor, i.e. the view of woman as a "pet" adored, pampered, and "maintained" (enslaved) for sexual amusement and satisfaction. This is why she is tied down, making her escape impossible. The staircase on which she is "perched," moreover, is symbolic of both a pedestal of veneration and a phallic structure. Her bodily posture is imitative of a woman who is sexually "on top."

Another possible interpretative line of reasoning is that of *woman-as-sacrificial-victim.* On top of a black altar, she is worshipped and offered as a sacrifice to the male god, Phallus. It is also relevant to note that the rope tied around her ankle is spermatozoic in shape and that it is colored red, a symbol of sexuality and eroticism. Is she tied in sexual bondage to some person, or to some irresistible force form below? The ambiguity of the rope's point of origin is powerful: the source of her enslavement may be the dark forces of nature, some dominating male, or even the woman herself. We will never know because the rope fades away into the dark background.

Let us now look at a few other visual cues that lead to other kinds of interpretations:

• The woman is barefoot, which is suggestive of fertility and of the woman's biological role as mother. The woman is, in fact, holding the bottle of Coco next to her face and breast, as she would a child.

• There is further ambiguity in the fact that the woman's bare back, shoulders, and scanty attire are highly erotic; but her slightly turned position is suggestive of modesty. The paradigmatic juxtaposition of eroticism and modesty give the woman great sexual allure.

• The oversized bottle of Coco, with its vivid amber color, juxtaposed against the dark background, is highly suggestive of fire and flames, and, thus, of burning desire.

As a final comment, it would seem that the woman is surrounded by a surreal void. The female "bird" appears mysteriously out of this nothingness, as in a dream. Is she a figment of the libidinous imagination? Is the subtext, therefore, simply that of an erotic dream which wearing the perfume, or buying it for your loved one, will make possible? Surrealism, as Bachand (1992: 5) remarks, "has been and still is a great inspiration to advertisers."

Advertisements as Art Forms

This ad, and Chanel advertisements and commercials generally, are always ambiguous and surreal. This is what gives them their great connotative force. Like traditional forms of visual art, they tap into underlying archetypal themes, instincts, and feelings that seek expression in symbolic form. A while back, Chanel had a commercial for the perfume Egoiste, showing a group of females (or was it the same female dressed in different clothes?) opening and shutting doors in a building and shouting égoiste over and over. Without going into the details of the commercial here, suffice it to say that its emotive force resided in its surreal and ambiguous quality: Were the women blaming men for their macho sexual egoism? Were they "opening" and "closing" their sexual organs?

Art can be thought of as a symbolic means for evoking fundamental feelings and affective states. The elicitation of feeling through symbolic forms is a powerful means for making meaning in the world and for extracting meaning from it. Art generally reveals a fascination with primordial consciousness. As mentioned above, children invariably start to draw as they discover their conscious thoughts. In adulthood, art penetrates the presentational level of mind, reawakening in us our now largely unconscious primordial feelings for the world around us. Thus, in a basic sense, the *Chanel* ads and commercials are works of "art." The difference between these works and, say, the works of a Rodin, a Renoir, or a Picasso is, in my view, that they are not "searching" for meaning to life. They are simply tapping into the unconscious domain of the mind in an attempt to associate its connotative dynamism, trivially, with a product.

In general, ads and commercials for perfume, clothes, drinks, and other lifestyle and "image-enhancing" products play on our hidden feelings. To enhance bodily image, or the bodily text we present to others, we resort typically to various forms of decoration or concealment. Underlying body image and especially the presentation of the face is, of course, the effect of sexual feelings. This is why the faces of models in ads and commercials are always crucial in getting the ad to work. Actually, the enhancement of the face, literally its "making up" for presentation, is as old as civilization itself. The cosmetic "make up" that we use today has a long and unbroken connection with ritualistic fertility behavior. It has a basis in sexuality: selecting colors, facial designs, and enhancements of facial features are all latent sexual signifiers in the facial text. Red lipstick appears to connote the redness associated with female genitalia; the wearing of mustaches by males can be easily seen to connote pubic hairs; and the list could on and on. The point to be made here is that the human face is hardly neutral semiotically. It is constantly being "made up" to convey messages ensconced in basic instinctual tendencies. As Helen Fisher (1992: 272-273) has aptly remarked, the sexually-constructed facial text is not a phenomenon restricted to modern humans. It probably was, as archeological evidence now seems to suggest, a characteristic feature of human bodily semiosis that goes right back to our Cro-Magnon ancestors. It seems that they too spent hours decorating themselves, plaiting their hair, donning garlands of flowers in order to smell sweet, wearing bracelets and pendants, and decorating their tunics and leggings with fur, feathers, beads, and red and yellow ocher. They also apparently strutted, preened, and showed off for one another around the fire's glow. So, if Fisher is right, the contemporary cosmetic and clothing fashion industries would seem to be linked to innate biological tendencies in the human organism that transcend time and culture. They are culturally-institutionalized reflexes of basic instincts, drives, and feelings.

Note the expression of the female in the *Coco* ad. She is staring tantalizingly at her prey, the viewer. Her face is a powerful carrier of sexual feeling states. As Paul Ekman (e.g. 1985 and 1988) has shown, the facial text can be broken down into its components: eyebrow position, eye shape, mouth shape, nostril size, etc. which in various combinations determine the expression of the face. It is, indeed, possible to write a "grammar" of the face which shows less cross-cultural variation than do language grammars. The features of the female's face are clearly representative of a sexual state of readiness and willingness. Note, as well, that the eye contact that the female is making with the viewer is particularly forceful as a sexual signifier. It may not be possible in the reproduction included here to see her pupils, but they appear to my perception, to be dilated. It is a documented fact by psychologists that the female face is perceived as more sexually attractive when the pupils are dilated. In fact, in earlier times in Italy, extracts of the drug *belladonna* were used for its cosmetic effect, given that it produces extreme dilation of the pupils. This drug is now used by eye doctors to facilitate eye examinations; but its cosmetic applications explain the origin of its name, which in Italian means "beautiful woman."

Perfume Advertisements

The foregoing analysis of the *Coco* ad constitutes an illustrative case-in-point of how iconic features can be analyzed to set up an interpretive frame through which it is possible to decode the ad at the subtextual level. As we have seen, the *Coco* ad recalls many of the themes in mythic literature about woman as predator and slave at the same time.

It should be stressed once again at this point that the interpretation of any specific ad or commercial starts with a consideration of the function of the product being advertised. The *Coco* ad, like the *Versus* and *Iron* ads, promotes a perfume product. In this chapter, and in the book generally, I have decided to focus on ads dealing with perfume, for the simple reason that these, more than most others, can be placed at the extreme connotative end of the interpretive continuum described in the previous chapter.

Perfume can be defined as an artifactual extension of the sexually-stimulating odors that are picked up by the olfactory system. At the biological level humans, like other animals, are responsive to odors and scents that they receive from the environment. The sense of smell is especially functional as a sexual stimulant in all animal species. Although the sense of sight has largely replaced the sense of smell for sexual arousal in humans — today we are more inclined to respond to erotic images than we are to bodily smells — the need for activating the olfactory sensory system at the more basic biological level does not go away.

So, perfume is definable semiotically as an artifactual surrogate for sexually-meaningful scent. Perfume works on the sexual emotions and is therefore quite apt to make a long lasting impression. Odors generally are mnemonically evocative. Years after our first infatuation we seldom fail to recognize a perfume fragrance that was worn by a loved one. This is because odor is often associated with a meaningful situation. A perfume fragrance can bring back vividly to mind a past situation and reawaken the corresponding feelings associated with it rather easily (Engen 1982). It has even been found that adults in a T-shirt experiment would value the body odor of their sexual partner as more pleasant and fragrant than the corresponding odor of a stranger (Schleidt 1980). Odors are also associated with meaningful spaces and places. We prefer the familiar "smell of home" to that of other abodes. We react negatively to the smell of places such as elementary schools, dental offices, etc. where we might have had unpleasant experiences.

Since bodily odors are stigmatized in contemporary industrialized societies, perfumes and deodorants have taken over as the primary stimuli of desirable olfactory responses. Our culture also makes categorical paradigmatic distinctions between "healthy" vs. "unhealthy," "sexy" vs. "unsexy," etc. in terms of specific kinds of scents. The perfume ad plays precisely on such paradigmatic dichotomies, defining sexuality in an artifactual way. Indeed, most perfume ads implicitly present their products as improvements on nature. As Vestergaard & Schrøder (1985: 159) remark, such ads proclaim their product as "somehow superior to their natural source," offering, in effect, "to lend nature a hand." The overall message transmitted by such ads is: "You too can be sexually attractive by simply wearing the fragrance of perfume X."

As is the case with all lifestyle products, perfume assumes a personality in advertising. Some perfumes are portrayed as "rugged" and "virile," like *Brut*; others as "smooth" and "refined," like *Chanel*. *Drakkar noir* obviously appeals to the dark, macabre, sinister side of masculine sexual fantasies. It is evocative of mythic portrayals like Don Juan, Dracula, and even Mephistopheles, the darkest of all. The guttural sound of *Drakkar* — obviously coined in imitation of *Dracula*, the deadly vampire who would mesmerize his sexual prey with a mere glance — is probably designed to evoke, unconsciously, both a surreptitious fear and a feeling of lust in the viewer. Is the *Drakkar noir* brand name alluding to the intertext of Faust selling his soul to the devil so that he could satisfy all his desires? Does wearing *Drakkar noir* constitute a Faustian pact with the devil to achieve erotic power? There is certainly much more to perfume than smell in this ad-mediated world!

A Methodological Summary

Dyer (1982) and others provide useful typologies of ads according to target audience. Clearly, an ad meant for a specialist in ophthalmology is going to be conceptualized and designed differently than a perfume ad meant for, say, today's upscale office worker. But there is general consensus among semioticians that lifestyle ads are the ones which generate the most meaning-intensive subtexts.

The following chart summarizes the main analytical procedures, or more accurately the "what to look for" items, to be employed in examining the iconic features of an advertisement text. The chart will be completed in the next chapter with the addition of a verbal decoding component. At the surface textual level, the analyst should, first and foremost, attempt to concatenate all the iconic cues into a coherent "narrative" of the ad. Then, these cues and the narrative should be assessed in terms of any subtextual connotations that are implicated. These are usually unconscious mythic and metaphorical themes that are linkable into an "open-ended" syntagmatic chain of connotations:

Surface Textual Level		Sub textual Level	
1. Iconic Decoding			
conscious		unconscious	
Look for	*Analytical Objective*	*Look for*	*Analytical Objective*
•visual-iconic cues and signifiers forming a "narrative" •other kinds of iconic features (e.g. the implied iconicity associated with the brand name, audio-oral features of any verbal contents, etc.)	•denotative meaning/and tentative guess at possible subtextual connotations inherent in the text	•mythic and metaphorical signifieds •any other conceptual structure	•syntagmatic chain of connotative meanings

In sum, decoding the underlying meaning of advertisements consists in correlating two orders of signification: (1) a surface textual, conscious, denotative one, and (2) a subtextual, unconscious, connotative one. Keep in mind that the connotative chain of association is formed only within a cultural context. The mythic themes and metaphors that are implied in the subtext fit into a coherent pattern of signification because the viewer is part of a cultural system of meaning which conceptualizes or understands a certain topic (sex, love, etc.) in specific mythical or metaphorical ways. As Alsted & Larsen (1991: 7-8)

aptly observe, lifestyle ads are "complex signifying texts" because they are grounded in a cultural substratum fertile with
mythic and metaphorical connotation.

A Few Other Illustrative Cases-in-Point

Consider, as another illustrative case-in-point, yet one other
Chanel ad which shows a woman standing on a park bench
holding a water hose, but dressed as if she were about to go out
"on the town," except for her casual shoes.[2] It is not necessary
to go here into a complete decoding of this ad. Only a few suggestive lines of inquiry will be followed.
     The first thing to do is to examine the iconic features of
the ad. Note that the background in the ad is that of a garden.
Now, ask yourself: Does this have any connotative meaning?
The answer is, of course, that in our culture, gardens frequently
have mythic connotations. Could this garden be suggestive of
the "Garden of Eden?" Let us, in fact, assume the hypothesis
that the subtextual level alludes to the temptation theme in
the Book of Genesis. Are there any other indications that this
is a plausible hunch? Look at what the woman is holding. It is
a hose in the form of a snake. Recall that the devil came to Eve
in the body of a snake to prod her on to tempt Adam. It would
seem that our working hypothesis is being corroborated iconically. Adam, of course, is the possessor of a phallus that
"ejaculates" in the same way that the hose does in the hand of
Eve. The "Garden of Eden" intertext in this ad and all its sexual-erotic connotations make it a psychologically powerful one.
Note as well the expression of satisfaction, domination, and
control on the face of the woman. One possible subtextual message implied by this facial schema is: "If you want to ensnare
your man, wear *Chanel* products and apparel, like Adam, he
will not be able to resist your charm." In a phrase, this ad can
be interpreted in terms of a mythic intertext — the Biblical
temptation theme. Given their prevalence, it would appear
that advertisers continually attempt to evoke such themes
perhaps because they reverberate effectively in the realm of
the subconscious *Id*.

---

2. Once again, we cannot provide an illustration because Chanel did not
   give permission to do so.

Consider, finally, the ads used to promote cigarettes. I cannot go into an analysis of specific ads here, mainly because I have found that cigarette companies deny permission to reprint their ads, perhaps because of the sensitivity to the smoking issue in society generally. So, I will make a few observations regarding an aspect of these ads, whose validity the reader can assay by examining them in any appropriate magazine.

Above all else, smoking constitutes a "performance" by which perceptions of masculinity and femininity are conveyed through bodily semiosis. The slow, circular movements of the arm in females are enactments of bodily schemas that our cultural perceives as "feminine." The abrupt movements employed by males, on the other hand, are performances of bodily schemas which are perceived as "masculine" by our culture. In all media images and representations, the female and male smoking performances show a paradigmatic structure that reflects differences in perceptions of gender: e.g. the female exhales the smoke in an upward direction, the male in a downward direction; the female's arm movements are slow and sultry, the male's are abrupt and rough; the female holds the cigarette in a tantalizing manner between the index and middle fingers, the male holds it in a stiff and rugged way between the thumb and middle finger, or else makes it dangle on the side.

In most of the cigarette ads and commercials in countries that are still allowed legally to show people actually smoking, the female's bodily schemas are, in a nutshell, portrayals of feminine sexuality (sensuality, voluptuousness, sultriness, etc.); the male's bodily schemas are representations of masculine sexuality (toughness, roughness, coarseness, etc.). As Erving Goffman (1979) argued a decade and a half ago, advertisements such as these portray the physical mode of male and female body schemas that reflect and reinforce traditional patterns of sex-role expectations. The cigarette always seems to take on a fetishistic quality, with rather obvious phallic connotations. It is portrayed as a sexual-erotic signifier that is manipulated unconsciously in paradigmatically complementary ways according to the sex of the smoker.

4

VERBAL FEATURES

Introduction

Recall how the wording of the *Iron* perfume ad (chapter 2), *Pump some iron*, was connected thematically to the iconic features of the ad, strengthening the syntagmatic links made among the various connotative meanings that the text educed: i.e. the expression was related, through *metaphor*, to the ad's subtext. This chapter will now focus on the skillful use of language in ads and commercials, and especially on the role that metaphorical language and concepts play in the subtext. Indeed, the analysis of advertisements reveals that most of the words and expressions employed are either structured metaphorically or else reflect some metaphorical concept.

The Metaphorical Basis of Concepts

Metaphor, it would seem, is a rather fascinating and unique feature of the human mind. Recall the *Miller* commercial of chapter 2 which ended with the metaphorical expression, *Love is a game*, appearing on the screen. Upon further reflection, it should become obvious that this statement is reflective of one of the ways in which our culture actually thinks about *love*. We seem, in fact, to perceive love and mating rituals as "games" to be played out according to specific rules.

Now, consider some of the expressions that we commonly use to talk about love (from Lakoff & Johnson 1980: 49):

(1) There were *sparks* between us.
(2) We are *attracted* to each other.
(3) My life *revolves* around her.
(4) I am *magnetically drawn* toward her.
(5) Theirs is a *sick* relationship.
(6) Their marriage is *dead*; it can't be *revived*.
(7) Their relationship is *in good shape*.
(8) I'm *crazy* about her.
(9) I'm constantly *raving* about him.
(10) He's gone *mad* over her.

(11) I've *lost my head* over him.
(12) She *cast* a spell over me.
(13) The *magic* is gone.
(14) She has *bewitched* me.
(15) I'm *in a trance* over her.

The first four sentences reveal that we commonly think of *love* as a physical force (gravitational, electromagnetic, etc.); sentences 5-7 indicate that we also think of *love* in terms of physical health and bodily states; sentences 8-11 disclose that we conceptualize *love*, at other times, as a mental state (madness); and sentences 12-15 reflect our perception of *love* as a kind of magical power or force. *Love* is indeed a *metaphor*, as the poets have always known! And this is not just a rhetorical statement, that is to say, metaphor is not just an ornamental feature of language, a decorative ploy for more basic speech and cognitive modes, as has been traditionally thought. It is a fundamental means by which we come to understand — to *conceptualize* — the world within and around us.

Consider more closely the notion of romantic *love*, to be distinguished conceptually, if not verbally, from other "kinds" of love. Throughout time, there probably has been no human being on the earth who has not *experienced*, to some degree, the feelings associated with *love*. But human beings the world over apparently *conceptualize* it differently in some way or other. At a biological level, the origin of the concept of romantic love is to be found, no doubt, in a recurrent pattern of instinctive responses to sexual stimuli such as increases in blood flow, muscle tension, emotional reactions, etc. which are registered as memorable by the mind. These patterns, known technically as *percepts*, constitute immediate units of knowing derived from sensation or feeling. Within the mind, however, these are reorganized into a *model* of feeling to which all humans intuitively identify and respond. At this level, what we call *love* is a perceived bodily and affective state. Then, through the workings of cultural sense-making, some of the constituents of this state are connected metaphorically to each other, or to other feelings, patterns, conditions and notions, to form the concept *love*. At this higher cognitive level *love* is *understood*, through metaphor, to be a physical force, a bodily state, a magical power, etc.

Consider the common conceptualization of love as a dulcet gustatory reaction: *You're so sweet, She's my sweetheart*, etc.

How did this originate? A plausible primal scenario is the following one. It could well be that our hominid ancestors associated their sexual feelings with some pleasant taste sensation derived from licking the face or other parts of the body during lovemaking. The association of affective state with gustatory reaction is easily forged by the human mind. The crystallization of the concept *love-as-a sweet taste* can, in my view, be traced phylogenetically to an associational process of this kind. It is, in fact, this very process which transferred the emerging feelings of what we have come to call *love* from the body to the world of mind. A *concept*, therefore, can be defined as any metaphorical connection made by the human mind within specific cultural contexts. So, we probably *feel* love in similar ways the world over, but we end up *thinking* about it in culture-specific ways. It is interesting to note that once a concept has been formed in this way it is not only coded within language, but it is the *raison d'être* of correlated cultural institutions and communal behaviors. Rituals of lovemaking in our culture invariably involve metaphorical thinking, such as the *love-is-sweet* metaphor: e.g. sweets are given to a loved one at St. Valentine's day; matrimonial love is symbolized at a wedding ceremony by the eating of a cake; we "sweeten" our breath with candy before kissing our loved one; etc.

Now, it is easy to understand why the *love-is-a game* metaphor employed by the makers of the *Miller* commercial is psychologically effective. Above all else, it reflects one of the ways in which we think about love, as the following common examples of discourse reveal:

(16) She left him, because he didn't *play by the rules*.
(17) He *lost* her to his best friend.
(18) She attempted to *win* his affections, but didn't.
(19) He didn't quite *score* with her the other night.
(20) Their love has lasted because they have always
     played on a even field

The *Miller* beer commercial clearly taps into this conceptual realm, and then structures its entire text around it. The actual statement of the metaphorical formula at the end of the commercial is, in effect, a verbal index pointing directly to this realm.

Cultural Models

How does *metaphor* work? Human beings are probably unique in continually trying to understand the inner world of the mind and emotions and the outer world of reality. We have been greatly aided in our quest for knowledge by our innate capacity to make signs. However, most of the time we are hardly "creative" thinkers. By and large, we literally let our culture "do the understanding" for us. We are born into an already-fixed system of signification built upon representational codes (language, gesture, etc.) and a communal memory system (traditions, laws, myths, scientific theories, etc.) that will largely determine how we will come to understand the world around us. This does not mean, however, that humans are incapable of thinking creatively and innovatively. On the contrary, we often question and challenge communal values, beliefs, etc. And, if all our communally-shared knowledge system were somehow to be effaced from the face of the earth, we would have the innate capacity to go right back to our primordial tendencies to literally *reinvent* the world all over again. Great thinkers and artists are revered, in fact, for their genius in thinking creatively and innovatively. Without them, cultures would become stagnant and moribund.

The foregoing discussion was meant primarily to emphasize how crucial the role played by culture — the totally human-made world of concepts, codes, artifacts, institutions, etc. — is in the formation of the human being. All knowledge systems are human inventions. This includes laws and scientific theories. But this does not mean, as the German philosopher Friedrich Nietzsche (1844-1900) despondently believed, that our inventions are no more than tokens of artifice or illusion and, therefore, that nothing is real. After all, the *theory* of aerodynamics is used rather successfully to fly planes; *theories* about cell structure and function allow doctors to cure various diseases; and so the list goes.

The ability to invent and represent the world semiotically actually enhances our survivability. The signs that we make and use all the time derive ultimately from having "sensed" and "felt" the world in some specific way. Inside the mind, we continually make connections among our sense-derived forms and patterns. These connections can then be "tried out," so to speak on the world. If they "work" as "conceptualized," it is because they are ultimately made up of the substance of sensation. We go from *sentio ergo sum* ("I feel, therefore I am") to the Cartesian state of *cogito ergo sum.* ("I think, therefore I am"). Our cogitations are "real" because they are derived ultimately from our biologically-determined survival modes of sensing and feeling. The ways in which a culture represents *love* affects the ways in which mating rituals unfold. For example, we feel that a love ritual of any kind must be initiated according to specific "rules of the game:" e.g. one of the two participants in the ritual is expected to initiate it; one of the two is expected to carry out various subroutines (initiate appropriate discourse, bring gifts to the other); and so on. But it must be kept in mind that what is considered appropriate mating behavior in one culture may not coincide with views of lovemaking in another. *Love* cannot be defined ahistorically, aculturally, or in purely absolutist terms. Lakoff & Johnson (1980) call the metaphorical ways in which we come to understand something like *love* as the specific *models* a culture forges to come to grips with reality. *Cultural modeling* is in large part a result of metaphorical thinking.

This perspective does not deny the existence of events and states in the body that will lead to "feeling" the sensations that we associate with love independently of cultural models of love. All organisms have an innate affective system that alerts them to changes in bodily states. But only in the case of the human organism are fluctuations in bodily functions seemingly grasped at a higher level and thus made available to reflective consciousness. Now, once a specific pattern of fluctuation has been selected and understood as *love,* then its converse becomes an immediate sign of *hate.* Problems in interpreting *love* and *hate* emerge typically when an individual comes from a culture in which these two states have not been conceptualized (in language, traditions, rituals, etc.) in identical ways.

The question now becomes: How do we come to conceptualize love in culturally-specific ways? Even a superficial consideration of this question will suggest that we do so through metaphorical thinking, As Lakoff & Johnson (1980) have cogently argued, a meticulous, detailed study of the metaphorical formulas employed by cultures will consistently reveals that they underlie the representation of most of our abstract concepts. The metaphors used in language are the signifying *reflexes* of the ways in which we think, and act.

Structurally, metaphor reveals an *A is B* underlying form. It mirrors a tendency of the human mind to think, or experience, one thing in terms of another. In the origin of a metaphor, the *A* is usually something abstract or unfamiliar, and the *B* something concrete or familiar. The model which has become the basic schema to discuss metaphor is the *topic-vehicle-ground* model put forward by Richards in 1936, and then refined by Wheelwright (1954) and Black (1962). After Black, this model has come to be known as the *interactional model*. The *topic*, also known as the *tenor*, is what is talked about in the metaphor (the *A-referent*). It is the thing that our mind literally wants to know more about. The *vehicle* is that part which makes a comment on the topic (the *B-referent*). It is the part that "explains" the *A* to us in terms of concrete or familiar notions. The *ground* is the meaning that is generated by the semantic *interaction* between tenor and vehicle. Thus, in the metaphor *time is money*, *time* is the tenor, *money* the vehicle, and the meaning — which would obviously require an extensive paraphrase — is the *ground*.

Recent work in linguistics and psychology has shown that metaphor operates at various levels of complexity and abstraction. *Seeing-is-knowing* is both a simple verbal metaphor, but also a much more encompassing cultural model of how we conceptualize *knowing* or *understanding*, as can be seen in the following examples:

(21) There is more to this than *meets the eye*.
(22) I have a different *point of view*.
(23) It all depends on how you *look* at it.
(24) I take a *dim view* of the whole matter.
(25) I never *see eye to eye* on things with you.

A little reflection should convince you that this embedded metaphorical pattern permeates many aspects of the way we think about *thinking*. This is why we constantly say that we have a *world-view*, *insight*, an *image* in our minds about something. So, at one level, the *seeing-is-knowing* formula is a convenient verbal metaphor. But at another level it is a cultural model of how *knowing* is perceived to unfold. In the framework of this model, the various metaphorical *vehicles* that instantiate this formula can take on any form, verbal and nonverbal. We say, for instance, that *justice is blind* and represent it by statues built outside or inside courtrooms with blindfolds to symbolize the vehicle. The metaphorical expression *scales of justice*, too, is commonly symbolized by corresponding sculptures of scales near or inside justice buildings. The instantiations of the vehicle are always evident in a discourse text, while the topic may or may not be mentioned. This view of metaphor extends it beyond the sentence level and the language system to encompass discourse, textuality, and cultural sense-making.

Although interest in metaphor is as old as Aristotle (384-322 BC), the experimental study of its relation to cognition and communication is a relatively recent phenomenon. Since the seventies interest in metaphor on the part of many scholars has become so intense that it is virtually impossible to skim even the surface of the empirical findings it has generated. What stands out most from this research domain is that metaphor is now viewed by many to constitute an intrinsic feature of how we represent the world and, subsequently, of how we construct cultural models of it. Indeed, without the capacity to metaphorize, culture would not exist.

Defining Metaphor

Metaphor evokes as many perceptions among people as it does definitions. Aristotle is the one who, in his *Rhetoric* and *Poetics*, coined the term — itself a metaphor (*meta* "beyond" + *pherein* "to carry") — to refer to the common verbal phenomenon of implicit comparison (*A implies B* or *A is B*). Aristotle's view has come to be known as the *comparison* theory of verbal metaphor. He noticed that language metaphors revealed something fundamental about the human mind: "Midway between the unintelligible and the commonplace, it is metaphor which most produces knowledge." However, Aristotle did not pursue this line of thinking. He simply acknowledged that metaphorical language was psychologically powerful, but affirmed that it was, in essence, an ornamental or stylistic option to more basic literal ways of thinking and speaking.

The literalist view of meaning has survived practically unaltered since Aristotle's time. It posits that metaphors are derivatives of more fundamental literal, propositional modes of cognizing. Some go even further, viewing metaphors as *deviations* from semantic rules. But in the last few decades such views of metaphor have come increasingly under attack. Since the seventies the scientific investigations of metaphor have been proliferating. In 1977, for instance, a study by Pollio and his associates (Pollio, Barlow, Fine, & Pollio 1977) showed that metaphorical language was an all-pervasive force in cognition and communication. They found that speakers of English uttered, on average, 3,000 novel verbal metaphors and 7,000 idioms per week. It became clear from their study that verbal metaphor was hardly a mere stylistic option to literal language. Since 1977 the number of volumes, symposia, courses and article-length studies on metaphor in the cognitive and social sciences has reached astronomical proportions.

Literalist and deviationist models of verbal metaphor are of no particular relevance here. Both claim, essentially, that literal speech is primary and that metaphors are extensions, deviations, or anomalies. As mentioned, this view is really no longer tenable. Aristotle's comparison theory is still, in my opinion, the basis for any discussion of metaphor. Over the course of the centuries, the Aristotelian model has been rejected or expanded. But its basic premise, expressed in the formula *A is B*, has never been completely discarded. The comparison view implies an analogy, or connection, between two concepts or entities.Verbal metaphor is construed, in effect, to be a condensed simile. Similarly, so-called *substitution* theories, which are versions of comparison theories, assume metaphor to be a form of *analogical* thinking that is useful for remedying gaps in literal expression. The comparison and substitution explanations of metaphor can be seen, in actual fact, to offer different perspectives on the same phenomenon. The metaphorical capacity does indeed inhere in the ability to *establish* similarities among phenomenologically-dissimilar things — at times by comparison, at others by substitution — to create models of the world that the mind can utilize in many diverse ways. Metaphor is a "tool" that the mind constantly enlists to explore reality and to give order and coherence to our otherwise chaotic experiences. In fact, metaphor can be said to fabricate similarity and resemblance in the world of human experience. The only way we can conceptualize "similarity" or "resemblance" is metaphorically!

Giambattista Vico (the Neapolitan philosopher mentioned in the previous chapter) defined *metaphor* as a "fable-making" capacity that allowed the first humans to make connections and, therefore, to literally create new, context-free associations. The primordial function of metaphor for Vico inhered in what the philosopher Donald P. Verene calls an "isness" relation (Verene 1981: 60-100). Traditionally, metaphor has been viewed as tied to analogy, i.e. as an operation that makes out something to be "like" something else. For Vico, on the other hand, the primordial operation of the metaphorical capacity established an "isness" among things, hence reifying them (i.e. bringing them into existence in a new way). Lakoff & Johnson (1980) relate mental imagery to metaphor by means of what they call *image-schema* theory. Johnson (1987: 79) defines *image schemas* as "those recurring structures of, or in, our perceptual interactions, bodily experiences and cognitive operations." For Lakoff (1987: 444) *image schemas* involve a largely unconscious process that portrays locations, movements, shapes, etc. in the mind in a systematic, patterned fashion. Lakoff (1987: 444-446) illustrates image-schema theory as follows. If someone is asked to explain an idiom such as *spill the beans* in terms of its associated imagery-content — "Where are the beans before they are spilled?" "How big is the container?" "Is the spilling on purpose or accidental?" etc. — then, Lakoff suggests, even those speakers who claim not to have a conscious image of the idiom can answer such questions in remarkably uniform ways: e.g. the beans are supposed to be kept in a container; the container is always described as being about the size of the human head; etc.

Now, as a further example of how verbal metaphors reveal an underlying cultural modeling process, take the concept of *time* as it is reflected in the following statements:

(26) I'm *wasting* too much time.
(27) That will *save* you hours.
(28) I've *invested* a lot of time in her.
(29) That mistake *cost* me several hours.
(30) He's living on *borrowed* time.

What these statements reflect is the value that money has in our culture; they reveal, in other words, the model *time-is-money*. This cultural model of time is intrinsically intertwined with similar models — *time-is-a-limited resource, time-is-a-valuablecommodity* — to produce increasingly complex conceptualizations of *time*. This is how abstract conceptualization seems to work in human beings. A *caveat* is in order at this point. The foregoing discussion in no way is meant to imply that all human concepts are metaphorical in origin and nature. Indeed, the prevalence of iconic and indexical signs is evidence that we form concepts in other ways as well. But, it is accurate to say that a large portion of our abstract notions — love, hope, honor, honesty, etc. — are forged metaphorically.

Metaphor and Metonymy

The study of metaphor has fallen traditionally within the discipline of *rhetoric*, the field that studies the techniques used in all kinds of discourses, from ordinary conversation to verbal aesthetic texts. Within this domain, metaphor is viewed to be one of the many *tropes* — figures of speech — to be studied. But, if the recent work in psychology and linguistics is correct, then *metaphor* is much more than "just a metaphor." This is why the practice today is increasingly to use this term to refer to the study of *all* figurative language and to consider the other tropes as particular kinds, or stylistically-shaped manifestations, of metaphor. Within this new analytical framework, *personification*, or the figurative endowment of inanimate objects or qualities with human attributes ("Life has caught up with him"), for instance, can be easily seen to have the general *A is B* structure. In this case the underlying conceptual structure is always *A-is-a person*. The same kind of reasoning can be applied to most of the other classical tropes — catachresis, hyperbole, etc.

But there is one type of metaphorical process that is regularly considered separately from metaphor. This is called *metonymy*, or the use of an entity to refer to another that is related to it. Here are some examples of this interesting phenomenon (Lakoff & Johnson 1980: 35-40):

(31) She likes to read *Dostoyevski* (= the writings of Dostoyevski).
(32) He's in *dance* (= the dancing profession).
(33) My mom frowns on *blue jeans* (= the wearing of blue jeans).
(34) New *windshield wipers* will satisfy him (= the state of having new wipers).

There is a special subtype of metonymy, known as *synecdoche*, which is particularly productive in cognition. This is the signifying process by which the part represents the whole:

(35) The *automobile* is destroying our health (= the collection of automobiles).

(36) We need a couple of *strong bodies* for our teams (= strong people).

(37) I've got a new *set of wheels* (= car).

(38) We need *new blood* in this organization (= new people).

Particularly fruitful in our culture is the metonymic formula *the face-is-the person:*

(39) He's just another *pretty face.*

(40) There are an awful lot of *faces* in the audience.

(41) We need some new *faces* around here.

This metonymic concept also crystallizes in nonverbal behaviors. It underlies the reason why portraits, in painting and photography, focus on the face. We look at a person's face first, and preparing and decoding the face is a primary act of signification. In fact, expressions such as *saving face, face the music,* etc. highlight the prominent role the face has as a metonym for personality.

To recapitulate, the foregoing discussion was designed to impress upon the reader that *metaphor* is hardly a verbal accessory, but a fundamental modeling ability in human cognition and culture. Advertisers seem to know this rather well, for at the core of their creative technique is metaphor. The specific cultural model enlisted may be expressed explicitly, as in the *Miller* commercial, or more often than not, left unexpressed and embedded in the subtext.

Metaphor in Advertisements

To illustrate how metaphor operates in advertising, consider two ads as illustrative cases-in-point: one for the perfume *Volupté* (fig. 8) and the other for *L'Effleur* fragrance products (fig. 9). *Volupté* is aimed at young women in their twenties and thirties. Perfume, as mentioned in the previous chapter, is a surrogate for sexually-stimulating odor. The reason for wearing perfume is, as a television commercial for *Impulse* blurted out a while back, self-explanatory: "If a man you don't know suddenly gives you flowers, that's *Impulse!*" This statement contains an interesting wordplay on the brand name of the perfume product. In the commercial, the woman appears pleased to receive the flowers

Fig. 6 — Ad for *Volupté* Perfume

Fig. 7 — Ad for *L'Effleur* Fragrance Products

from a stranger (as shown by her smile), and the man uses his sense of smell, and his own masculine *impulse*, to make his way through a crowd of people to locate the female that he remembers having smelled.

The bottle of *Volupté* is located in the center of the ad text, which, of course, gives the bottle focus and salience. The very name of the perfume is the first interpretive key to its subtext: it is French for "voluptuous." So, what does the phrase *Trust your senses*, placed just below the perfume bottle, imply? At a denotative level, this can be seen to refer to the sense of smell, since that is what perfume is designed to stimulate. But, then, the shape of the perfume bottle leads the viewer, subtextually, to enlist his/her other senses as well. One possible iconic interpretation of the bottle is that of a female breast: it has a dark, round center reminiscent of a nipple. The nipple can indeed be seen and felt. The viewer, male or female, knows subconsciously that an "aroused nipple" is a sign of successful sexual foreplay.

The sense of sight is also enlisted in the juxtaposition of the dark background and the "beam" of white light that spotlights the "object" of sensuality. This *chiaroscuro* effect is evocative of awe and veneration. Now, ask yourself, where have you seen this kind of scene? Of what is it reminiscent? What feelings does it elicit?

Let's attempt a few guesses. As mentioned several times before, darkness in our culture connotes fear, evil, the unknown. This is why we talk of "black masses." The placement of the bottle in the middle of the ad could in fact be interpreted to suggest an "altar" setting or a stage scene for some kind of erotic performance; it is highly suggestive, in other words, of an illicit or taboo performance/ritual being conducted in the darkness. The sexually-evocative name of the perfume, *Volupté*, reinforces our feeling that something forbidden, but nevertheless appealing, is about to happen. It's as if the bottle were being worshipped on an altar or stage. Perfume is, of course, worn with one specific goal in mind — to enhance one's sexual attractiveness. Sexual activity, moreover, is normally conducted in the dark. The verbal part of the text, *Trust your senses*, reinforces this mode of interpretation, since in the dark one must indeed trust one's senses to locate the object of desire. Only because of the beam of light in the midst of the dark is the sense of vision able to focus on the perfume bottle.

The beam is evocative of several possible scenarios: the turning on of the light after sexual intercourse; a symbolic sign "from above" warning us about the unholy paganism of sexual urges; a "breakthrough" in satisfying our lustful desires; a spotlight at an erotic performance; and the list could go on and on. Light is the paradigmatic opposite of dark.

Iconically, then, the scene in the *Volupté* ad suggests a secluded, dark place where the bottle (female sexuality) is to be worshipped, looked at voyeuristically, and then smelled. This scene, with its erotic connotations, is reinforced verbally by the phrase *Trust your senses*, which is grounded on an embedded cultural model: *the female body (e.g. her breasts) ås-an object of sexual desire.*

In the *L'Effleur* ad, which spotlights flowers in the shape of a heart, the metaphorical formula implicated would appear, instead, to be that of *love-is-a flower (sweet smell)*. This formula underlies such descriptions of love in our culture as something that *blossoms, sprouts, blooms, grows,* etc. The phrase in the ad *Somewhere inside, romance blossoms*, is tied thematically and conceptually to this cultural model. Here love is not *voluptuous*, but *romantic*. The other thematic areas encompassed by this ad are those of "innocence," "purity," "spirit-uality," as indicated by the woman's white dress, by the hug given to her by the little girl (a sign of innocent affection), and by the butterflies and angels embedded in the floral arrangement. In a phrase, the ad draws a picture of lovemaking as idyllic, bucolic, sentimental romance. Note also the fact that the woman is wearing a long dress which covers her flesh, thus deemphasizing the carnal aspects of love and emphasizing, instead, the romantic aspects. This picture is completed and reinforced by the little love poem about *First Love: Befitting and fragrant, we send bouquets, to the one who gave us yesterdays.*

Finally, note that the flower arrangement seems to be attached to a white gown, which is clearly suggestive of a wedding dress. The implied subtextual message is, of course: "If you want to marry your first love, make sure you wear *L'Effleur* products." Incidentally, both body products use French names, adding to their exotic appeal: erotic and sensual in the case of *Volupté*, blissful and pure in the case of *L'Effleur*.

It is interesting to note, by the way, how brand names are designed to work psychologically. As Wolfe (1989: 3) points out, brands with connotatively-rich names are effective at the unconscious level. For example, the perfume name *Poison*, by Christian Dior, has an immediate impact because "the apparent contradiction between product description or denotation — a lethal substance — and connotation — a seductive one" evokes "mystery, alchemy and the archetype of the sorceress" (Wolfe 1989: 3). Brand names of lifestyle products, as Dyer (1982: 141) remarks, certainly do more than just identify the product:

> The names given to cosmetics and other beauty products frequently recall images of beauty, cleanliness, sophistication and naturalness: Moondrops, Natural Wonder, Rainflower, Sunsilk, Skin Dew. Sometimes the names of products convey scientific authority: Eterna 27, Clinique, Endocil, Equalia. Men's toiletries (not "beauty products," you notice) also have evocative names: Brut, Cossak, Denim, Aramis, Devin. And it doesn't take much imagination to work out why cigarette brands are called by such names as Piccadilly, Embassy, Sovereign, Consulate, State Express, Lambert and Butler, nor why there are cars called Jaguar, Mustang, Triumph, Princess.

Other Linguistic Features

Over three decades ago, the linguist Roman Jakobson (1960) put forward a model of communication that would seem to be particularly useful in describing the verbal features of ads and commercials. He posited six "constitutive" factors that make up any act of communication: (1) an *addresser*, or the sender of the message; (2) an *addressee*, or the individual for whom the message is intended; (3) a *message* to be communicated; (4) a *context*, or the recognition of the message as referring to something other than itself; (5) *contact*, by which he meant the physical channel in which a message is uttered and the psychological connections between the addresser and addressee; and (6) the *code*, or the shared system of signs and relations by which a text is constructed:

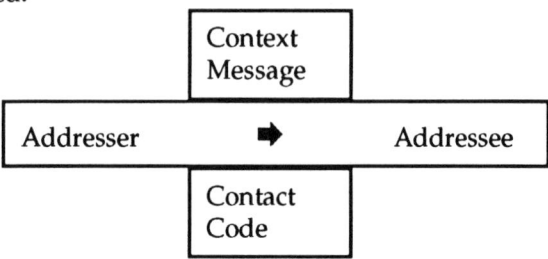

Fig. 8 — Jakobson's Constitutive Factors of Communication

Jakobson then argued that each of these constitutive factors determines a different communicative function of language. According to Jakobson, there are six such functions:

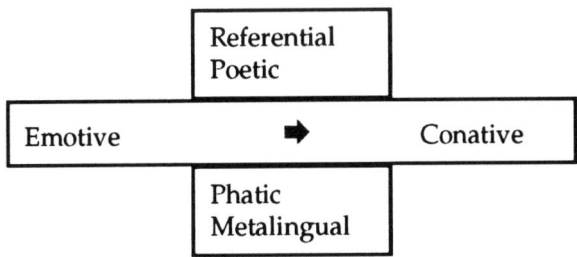

Fig. 9 —Jakobson's Communicative Functions

The *emotive* function refers to the fact that an addresser's emotions, attitudes, social status, etc. shape the construction of his/her verbal text. The emotive function varies in degree according to type of message: poetic texts, for example, tend to be more emotive than referential ones. The effect — physical, psychological, social, etc. —that the verbal text has on the addressee is the *conative* function. The types of verbal texts that we construct can be *referential, poetic, phatic,* and *metalingual.* A *referential* text is a straightforward exchange of information ("Bloor Street is two blocks north of here"); a *poetic* text is aesthetically-constructed ("Roses are red, violets are blue, so how's it going with you?"); a *phatic* text allows for the establishment of contact ("Hi, how's it going?"); and a *metalingual* text is a verbal text that refers to itself or identifies the code being used ("This book is about semiotics").

In Jakobsonian terms, it can be said that an advertisement *communicates* something only if the addresser (the ad/commercial creators) uses a code to which the addressee (the targeted audience) has access. Moreover, it can be said that the advertising's subtextual message involves the deployment of appropriate contextual and contact features that will maximize its conative effect on the addressee. The use of poetic language (metaphor, rhythm, rhyme, etc.) will increase the conative impact of an advertising message. This is, no doubt, why ad writers often use *alliteration,* or the repetition of sounds, for various effects (*sing-song; no-no,* etc.); sound-modeling effects (*Zap!, Boom!, Pow!,* etc.); and other rhetorical devices. But advertisers will also employ other Jakobsonian functions to make their messages emotive, such as the phatic one: *Have a good day, at McDonald's.* Recently, Fries (1993) has documented statistically that phrases used to describe the product are invariably structured syntactically and communicatively to focus the greatest amount of attention on the brand name. Moreover, the use of poetic language as Bachand (1992: 3) puts it, is "expressly designed to incorporate (accentuate) the [brand] name into the system of daily life." Jingles such as *Join the Pepsi generation*, quickly make their way into daily discourse and into our communal memory.

In television and radio commercials, there are several audio-oral features tied to the subtextual level which the semiotician should always keep in mind when decoding: e.g. the tone of voice, the sentence structure, and the use of various word ploys (see also Dyer 1982: 141-150). The tone of voice can be seductive, friendly, cheery, insistent, foreboding, etc. as required by the subtextual themes of the commercial. The sentence structure of ads and commercials is usually informal and colloquial, unless the ad is about some "high-class" product (e.g. a *BMW* automobile, a *Parker* pen, etc.), in which case it is normally more elegant and refined. In general, the type of sentence used in ads is, as we have seen, a short imperative phrase — *Pump some iron, Trust your senses* — or aphoristic statement — *Somewhere inside, romance blossoms*. Advertising also borrows discourse styles to suit its purposes: a commercial can take the form of an interview, a testimonial on the part of a celebrity, an official format (*Name:* Mary; *Age:* 15; *Problem:* acne); and so on.

Rhetorical devices are common in advertising. These, too, can be used as templates for decoding subtextual meanings. Here are three frequently-used kinds (Dyer 1982: 151-182):

•*Tautologies.* Ad writers often make statements that are meaningless but enunciated as necessarily true: *Triumph has a bra for the way you are; A Volkswagen is a Volkswagen;* etc.

•*Tropes.* As discussed above, figurative statements in advertisements allow for the build-up of an associational system for the product: *Come to where the flavor is...Marlboro country* (metaphor);*Bring a touch of Paris into your life* (metonymy); etc.

•*Repetition.* The repetition of sounds or patterns is an effective memory strategy. *Parallelism* is the repetition of linguistic patterns (sentences, phrases, etc.): *It's longer/It's slimmer/It's surprisingly mild* (advertisement for *More* cigarettes). *Alliteration* is the repetition of the initial consonant sounds or features of words —*The Superfree sensation; Guinness is good for you;* etc.

•*Absence of language.* Some ads strategically avoid the use of any language whatsoever, suggesting, by implication, that the product speaks for itself. As Dyer (1982: 170) puts it, the absence of language in certain ad texts "has the effect of making us think that meaningful reality lies directly behind the signs once we have succeeded in deciphering them." A particularly skillful use of this type of technique is *preterition*, or intentional omission, which can be seen in ads that purportedly tell a secret: *Don't tell your friends about...; Do you know what she's wearing?;* etc.

A Methodological Summary

The analysis of the metaphorical and verbal features of the advertisement text leads to a completion of the interpretive guide started in the previous chapter. In essence, the verbal component of an ad text — product name, accompanying phrases, etc. — generally reinforces the subtext's syntagmatic chain of connotation:

Surface Textual Level		Subtextual Level	
1. Iconic Decoding			
conscious		*unconscious*	
Look for	*Analytical Objective*	*Look for*	*Analytical Objective*
•visual-iconic cues and signifiers forming a "narrative" •other kinds of iconic features (e.g. implied iconicity associated with the brand name, audio-oral features of any verbal contents, etc.)	•denotative meaning/and tentative guess at possible connotations inherent in the text	•mythic and metaphorical signifieds •any other conceptual structure	•syntagmatic chain of connotative meanings

2. Verbal Decoding			
conscious		*unconscious*	
Look for	*Analytical Objective*	*Look for*	*Analytical Objective*
•special features or meanings of brand name	•complementing that denotative meaning	•methaphorical formulas and cultural models	•reinforce the syntagmatic chain of connotative meanings
•any statements or words that are given/ spoken		•any other linguistic feature or rhetorical device	

5

CONCLUDING REFLECTIONS

Introduction

The primary goal of this guide has been to describe a semiotic method for interpreting (decoding) lifestyle advertisements. This brief chapter is more reflective and philosophical. Its purpose is to offer my own perspectives on the "meaning" and "effects" of advertising in our society.

Postmodern Culture

Today's world has often been characterized as a *postmodern* culture; i.e. as a culture that has lost faith in the progressive social and technological achievements that led to the *modern* world's scientific sophistication and self-assurance. Its mode of cognizing has been described by social critics as ironic, nihilistic, surreal. Human actions are not perceived to have some ulterior purpose, but to be essentially meaningless. Lifestyle advertising is, in my view, definable as a form of postmodern communication, a discourse that mirrors how contemporary humans in the mass perceive reality — as a collage of lifestyle images that reflect basic drives, desires, and sexual experiences.

Late twentieth-century humans have largely abandoned hope in the existence of worlds other than the present one. We appear, by and large, to be skeptical and cynical about the "meaning" of human existence. We feel that there really is nothing "out there," that everything is an illusion, and that life is a momentary state of consciousness on its way to extinction.

But there is, paradoxically, a countervailing force that is also shaping our fractured psyche. On a deeper intuitive level we seem to be constantly and desperately hoping that there is a "plan" to existence, and that our otherwise senseless actions can be tied together in a teleologically meaningful way. Like the six characters in Luigi Pirandello's 1921 play, *Six Characters in Search of an Author*, we seem today to urgently need to continue our search for an author to write us into existence. The search may lead errantly to televangelism, cults, pseudo-meditation sects, and the like, but more often than not it is leading to a profound reevaluation of the meaning of consciousness and particularly of the concept of the human spirit. At a more profound level we seem to sense that there is a spiritual reality that can only be felt, not understood.

The *modern* perspective originated in the Renaissance and was reinforced in the Age of Reason. *Modern* cultures have always put their faith in human reason and in its intellectual offspring — science and logic: i.e. unlike medieval cultures, they have never searched for the design and meaning of reality solely in the words of God, but in the discoveries of science and in the theoretical creations of the logical mind. In other words, the modern mind has always believed that the world is self-contained and can be perfectly well understood by the methods of science without reference to supernatural explanations. But like the medieval mind, modern cultures have never eliminated the need for believing in God, having always felt that God is at the "center" of the universe, that God is ultimately the "author" of the cosmological and human worlds that the mind seeks to understand through reason.

In the eighteenth century, the dizzying growth of technology and the constantly-increasing certainty that science could eventually solve all human problems — perhaps even prolong life indefinitely by discovering the "life principle" and thus conquering death — brought into existence a new form of mentality. By the end of this century, the now famous assertion that "God is dead" by the German philosopher Friedrich Nietzsche (1844-1900) both acknowledged that the modern mind had run its course and that a new worldview had crystallized — a worldview that had lost its belief in anything beyond the immediate material form of existence.

The term *postmodernism* came out of the field of architecture to describe the eclectic, colorful variety of building styles that urban architects were beginning to design more and more in the seventies. Immediately after it was coined, the term caught on like wildfire in academic circles, and is now used to describe everything from contemporary paintings to the methods of artificial intelligence. *Postmodernism* can be defined simply as the worldview of late twentieth century urban culture that everything "out there" is a figment of the human mind. That there is no absolute truth in our histories and in our scientific theories. It is, therefore, a term that has come forward to nicely capture the view that all knowledge and history are expressions of the human mind, not "discoveries" made by the mind.

In my view, there is little doubt that the contemporary version of the postmodern mind has been in large part fostered by our advertising-mediated culture. Viewing the world through a television camera or through magazine ads is bound, eventually, to lead to a perspective that Soomon (1988: 212) aptly characterizes as "perceptual montage." This means that we tend at times to gaze upon the world as if it were a TV program or a scene in an ad. Day in and day out these fragmented images of life are bound to influence our overall view that reality is illusory, surreal as in the *Coco* or the *Versus* ads discussed in previous chapters. Ultimately, we are led to form the view that human actions are a montage of disconnected images, desires, feelings, etc.

Language in the postmodern mind takes on a new modality of representation: it is either imbued with irony or else it is reduced to mere verbal recipes, stock phrases, and the kind of formulaic discourse that ads constantly promulgate. It is not tied to a larger social, religious, or philosophical narrative. It is instantaneous, satisfying immediate desires. The postmodern mind is ahistorical and nihilistic. As the sociologist Zygmunt Bauman (1992: vii-viii) has perceptively remarked, postmodernism is "a state of mind marked above all by its all-deriding, all-eroding, all-dissolving *destructiveness.*"

Advertising as New Discourse

Traditionally, the religious forms of discourse — gospels, catechisms, sacred books, etc. — have always had, as one of their intents, the promulgation of the "good news" about the origin, development, and destiny of humanity. This is in fact the meaning of the word *gospel*. Today, the good news, as Bachand (1994: 144) aptly claims, "is being announced by advertisers." Advertising now constitutes a form of discourse that celebrates consumption; it is the liturgy of consumerism. But this new catechism has no "divine author" with meaningful "answers to life." Its discourse categories merely announce that: "If you buy this or that, then you will be eternally young, sexy, happy, etc." No wonder, then, that mythic-religious themes — recall the mythic imagery implicit in the subtexts of the ads examined in previous chapters —

pervade modern advertising. What is implicit in the advertising discourse is consumeristic prophecy — a postmodern replacement of eschatological prophecy which once proclaimed the immanence of the afterlife in the present world. As Bachand (1994: 146) eloquently puts it: "The product literally seems like a creation emerging from the depths of formless matter to provide endless satisfaction."

As Spitzer (1979) has noted, it is ironic to contemplate that traditional Protestantism may have been the motivating force behind advertising's evolution and installment, since it has always encouraged the accumulation of goods in the world. As a consequence, it has unwittingly legitimized the contemporary discourse of advertising. The advertiser has, in a basic social sense, taken over the role of the preacher, promulgating the good news and the constant need to improve oneself. As Bachand (1994: 147) states: "There is a sermon in each advertisement; and all advertisers devote themselves to proclaiming their faith and the means of attaining paradise on earth through consumption and, in the meantime, through communication."

How did this all come about? Nietzsche's nihilistic prediction that "God was dead" meant, of course, that everything in human belief systems, including religious beliefs, can be seen by the reflective mind to be no more than constructions of that very mind. By the early part of the twentieth century the view that history had a purpose which was "narrated," so to speak, by a divine source (as, for example, in the Western Bible) was coming increasingly under attack. At mid-century, Western society was starting to become increasingly more "deconstructive," i.e. more inclined to take apart the structures — moral, social, and mental — that had been shaped by this narrative. By the sixties, Western society had become fully entangled in a postmodern frame of mind, believing more and more that human beings fulfill no particular purpose for being alive, that life is a meaningless collage of actions on a relentless course leading back to nothingness.

Now, not everyone in our culture thinks in this way. There are many who, as a matter of fact, react against this kind of outlook. But it is becoming symptomatic of increasingly larger sectors of the culture. And, in my view, advertising has become the discourse form that reflects this cultural "symptomatology." Image-making has now become fully externalized in the form of products manipulated by media specialists. Television and advertising have become the postmodern mind's imagination and language. But the advertiser's imagination and his/her language typically fail to make a distinction between imagery and information on the one side, and true knowledge and wisdom on the other.

Advertising as "Poetry"

Advertising has become a kind of cultural *meta-language*, synthesizing verbal and nonverbal elements into a "compressed" textuality that sends out its message instantly, effortlessly, sensorially. As discussed previously, the magazine ad, for instance, can be viewed as contemporary *art* form, given that art of any type is a code-based form of representation that converts sense and feeling structures into signifying cultural texts. Magazine advertising is psychologically powerful because it combines the visual mode of representation (as do the fine arts) with the verbal one (as do the literary arts). As Henri Lefebvre (1968: 202-203) has put it, advertising has become the "poetry" of contemporary society, seizing "art and literature, with all available signifiers and vacant signifieds." As Bachand (1994: 134) also observes, since "ordinary" people today do not engage in "serious" reading or philosophical contemplation by and large, it should come as little surprise to find that advertising has come forward to provide "an opportunity for varied aesthetic experience." This is why the writer Georges Jean (1966: 82) remarked a few decades ago that advertising has come forward to fill the "need for poetry which exists in every human being."

Bachand (1994: 135) puts this whole line of reasoning in perspective as follows:

> Thus advertising reinterprets the elements of semiological heritage in its own way, while taking modern sensibilities into account. It combines and transforms the processes and content of communication and thus participates in the updating and revival of the classical forms of expression.

No wonder, then, that advertising is being acknowledged as art more and more; having even its own category of prize at the Cannes film festival. Although we may superciliously be inclined to condemn its objectives, as an aesthetic-inducing experience we invariably enjoy it. Advertisements convince, please, and seduce. Advertising works aesthetically. And it is adaptive, constantly seeking out new forms of expression reflecting fluctu-ations in social trends and values. Not only, but its forms have even been adapted and coopted by mainstream artists and writ-ers. Some pages of the contemporary writer Jean Marie Gustave Le Clézio, for instance, reveal an amalgam of traditional literary expression and advertising styles and forms. As Bachand (1994: 143) states, in this way "a dialectic of recuperation and diversion is developed, and through it the different semiotic systems that constitute the prevailing social imagination are refracted."

But there is a fundamental difference between the great works of art that all cultures identify as "saying something" about life and advertising. The goal of the great artists has al-ways been to imbue our universal human experience with meaning and sense of purpose. The great works of visual art, the great dramas, the great music of *all* cultures, not just the Western one, are meant to transform the experience of human feelings and events into memorable works that transcend time and cul-ture. Advertising, on the other hand, communicates nothing of any lasting or profound value, but trendy, "cool" attitudes and images. This new artistic vernacular constitutes a means aimed at grabbing the attention of a generation of individuals with seemingly reduced attention spans. Advertising is the art of the trivial, quickly becoming all too familiar and boring.

Advertising: A Semiotic and Psychological Synopsis

In this postmodern world, all is not lost, as Nietzsche so glumly predicted. I may be perhaps overly optimistic, but I believe that the human spirit will prevail, and that our postmodern culture will eventually redefine and reconstitute itself. As mentioned in the opening chapter, I believe that it is unlikely that people are victimized by advertising, as many psychologists would claim. Children and teenagers are more influenced to act by their fami-lies and by their peers than they are by media images. In my opinion, there is no causal link between television violence, for instance, and violence in society in general. Did television en-gender the wars fought throughout history, including the two devastating world wars in this century? Did it spur Jack the Ripper to slash his victims to death? Was it responsible for all the horrendous crimes perpetrated in the name of religion, nation-hood, and the like? Of course it didn't. It makes no sense whatsoever to think of television and advertising as instigators of specific kinds of aberrant behaviors. If that were so, then this principle would apply to all media, codes, and texts, including religious ones. What is more accurate to say is that the general *modus pensandi* and lifestyle models of our culture are reflected in the textuality of advertisements.

Even though we absorb the messages transmitted constantly by ads and commercials, and although these may have some unconscious effects on our behavior, we accept media images only if they suit our already-established preferences. If we complain about the shallowness of our television and advertising culture, we really have no one to blame but ourselves.

It is true, however, that advertising has probably contributed significantly to creating a desire for the lifestyles it portrays in other parts of the world. When asked about the stunning defeat of communism in eastern Europe, the Polish leader Lech Walesa was reported by the newspapers as saying that it all came from the television set, implying that television undermined the stability of the communist world's relatively poor and largely sheltered lifestyle with images of consumer delights seen in western programs and commercials. Different cultures have indeed been reshaped to the form and contents of television's textuality. Marshall McLuhan's phrase of the "global village" is still an appropriate one — television and advertising have shrunk the world and diminished the interval between thought and action.

Demographic surveys now show consistently that people spend more time in front of television sets than they do working, that watching TV is bringing about a gradual decline in reading, that television's textuality is leading to the demise of the nation state concept as ideas and images cross national boundaries daily through television channels. When the German printer Johann Gutenberg (1400?-1468?) invented movable type to print the Bible, he initiated a veritable revolution in human mental evolution and culture by making ideas readily available to a larger population. Television and advertising have triggered the twentieth century's own "Gutenberg revolution." But rather than homogenizing the world, it is my view that human diversity and ingenuity will lead to a greater variety in television programming and advertising and, therefore, in social textuality. As Solomon (1988: 124-125) aptly puts it, our "craving for variety is nature's way of providing us with an evolutionary edge in the struggle for survival in a constantly changing world."

Final Remarks

As I have attempted to show in this book, advertisements generate a truly interesting and rich array of connotations. These can be deciphered by analyzing the iconic and verbal cues of the surface ad text semiotically. Once the subtext has been decoded, the appeal of the ad seems to vanish, even in the case of highly connotative ads like the *Chanel* ones.

Thus, at the risk of sounding élitist, I believe that advertising will never be able to replace the traditional forms of artistic expression. These document humanity's search for meaning; their subtexts are open-ended and profound. Advertising, on the other hand, exploits our need for meaning trivially to enhance sales of a product. Many critics refer to the effects of advertising as *reification*, the process of encouraging people to identify their desires and needs with objects that can be bought and sold. Advertising seems no more just to advertise products, but to promote a way of life through reification. But we must not forget, as Leiss, Kline & Jhally (1990: 33) remind us, that blaming advertising is like blaming the messenger for the message: "Objections directed at advertisements, the industry, and its alleged social impacts are often indirect attacks on the so-called materialistic ethos of industrial society, or on capitalism in general as a social system; these are critiques of society masquerading as critiques of advertising."

In the end, it may be true that advertising may be reshaping the world in more ways than we might think, as some critics suggest. As I look at people shopping, at parties, driving down the road, sitting at an outdoor café sipping coffee, etc. I cannot help but see in their bodily schemas, in the way they wear their clothes, in the discourse they generate, etc. a reenactment of many of the images and scenes created by advertisers. I witnessed a striking example of this a few years ago when I attended a party of young upscale professionals. At a certain point during the evening, I saw an interactional scene that reminded me of a beer commercial that was popular on television at the time. The young men and women were posturing towards each other in ways that were almost identical to those of the actors in the television commercial. A culture mediated so pervasively by advertising images is asking for trouble. What Kubey & Csikszentmihalyi (1990: 199) have to say about the psychosocial effects of television applies, in my view, as well to advertising:

> Because consciousness is necessarily formed by exposure to information, media fare helps define what our most important and salient goals should be. Being an intimate part of the consumer society, television tells us that a worthwhile life is measured in terms of how many desirable material objects we get to own, and how many pleasures we get to feel. To achieve such goals complex skills are unnecessary. Even though some people spend a great deal of attention in trying to find bargains, in monitoring prices and sales, in developing culinary taste and fashion sense, in keeping abreast of new models and new gadgets, for the most part consumption does not require much disciplined effort and therefore does not produce psychological growth.

The answer to the dilemma of advertising is not to be found in censorship or in any form of state control of media and information. Even if it were possible in a consumerist culture to control the contents of advertising, this would invariably prove to be counterproductive. The answer is, in my view, to become aware of the subtexts that ads and commercials generate with the help of semiotic analysis. When the human mind is aware of the hidden codes in texts, it will be better able to fend off the undesirable effects that such texts may cause. As Drummond (1991: 7) has put it, semiotics can help to demystify advertising creativity and make "the process of meaning creation more accessible."

REFERENCES

Albion, M. & Farris, P. (1981). *The Advertising Controversy*. Boston: Auburn House.

Alsted, C. & Larsen, H. H. (1991). Choosing Complexity of Signs in Ads. *Marketing Signs* 10: 1-14.

Anderson, M. (1984). *Madison Avenue in Asia: Politics and Transnational Advertising*. Cranbury, N. J.: Associated University Presses.

Andren, G. L., Ericsson, L., Ohlsson, R., & Tännsjö, T. (1978). *Rhetoric and Ideology in Advertising*. Stockholm: AB Grafiska.

Arnheim, R. (1969). *Visual Thinking*. Berkeley: University of California Press.

Atwan, R. (1979). *Edsels, Luckies and Frigidaires: Advertising the American Way*. New York: Dell.

Bachand, D. (1994). The Art of (in) Advertising: From Poetry to Prophecy. in Mediating Culture. The Politics of Representation. William Anselmi and Kosta Gouliamos (Ed), Montréal/New York: Guernica, 133-150.

Barnouw, E. (1978). *The Sponsor: Notes on a Modern Potentate*. Oxford: Oxford University Press.

Barthel, D. (1988). *Putting on Appearances: Gender and Advertising*. Philadelphia: Temple University Press.

Barthes, R. (1957). *Mythologies*. Paris: Seuil.

Barthes, R. (1967). *Système de la mode*. Paris: Seuil.

Barthes, R. (1968). *Elements of Semiology*. London: Cape.

Barthes, R. (1977). *Image-Music-Text*. London: Fontana.

Bauman, Z. (1992). *Intimations of Postmodernity*. London: Routledge.

Bell, S. (1990). Semiotics and Advertising Research: A Case Study. *Marketing Signs* 8: 1-6.

Bendinger, B. (1988). *The Copy Workshop Workbook*. Chicago: The Copy Workshop.

Berger, A. A. (1984). *Signs in Contemporary Culture: An Introduction to Semiotics*. Salem: Sheffield.

Bergin, T. G. & Fisch, M. H. (1984). *The New Science of Giambattista Vico*. Ithaca: Cornell University Press.

Black, M. (1962). *Models and Metaphors*. Ithaca: Cornell University Press.

Campbell, J. (1969). *Primitive Mythology*. Harmondsworth: Penguin.

Courtenoy, A. E. & Whipple, T. W. (1983). *Sex Stereotyping in Advertising*. Lexington, Mass.: Lexington Books.

Cox, M. (1992). *Children's Drawings*. Harmondsworth: Penguin.

Danesi, M. (1994). *Messages and Meanings: An Introduction to Semiotics*. Toronto: Canadian Scholars' Press.

Danna, S. R. (1992). *Advertising and Popular Culture: Studies in Variety and Versatility*. Bowling Green, Ohio: Bowling Green State University Popular Press.

Driver, J. C. & Foxall, G. R. (1984). *Advertising Policy and Practice*. New York: Holt, Rinehart and Winston.

Drummond, G. (1991). An Irresistible Force: Semiotics in Advertising Practice. *Marketing Signs* 10: 1-7.

Dyer, G. (1982). *Advertising as Communication*. London: Routledge.

Eco, U. (1976). *A Theory of Semiotics*. Bloomington: Indiana University Press.

Ekman, P. (1985). *Telling Lies*. New York: Norton.

Ekman, P. (1988). Moving Faces: Facial Expressions and Emotion. *International Semiotic Spectrum* 10: 1-3.

Elliot, B. (1962). *A History of English Advertising*. London: Batsford.

Engen, T. (1982). *The Perception of Odours*. New York: Academic.

Enninger, W. (1992). Clothing. In: R. Bauman (ed.), *Folklore, Cultural Performances, and Popular Entertainments*, pp. 123-145. Oxford: Oxford University Press.

Ewen, S. (1976). *Captains of Consciousness*. New York: McGraw-Hill.

Ewen, S. (1988). *All Consuming Images*. New York: Basic.

Fisher, H. E. (1992). *Anatomy of Love*. New York: Norton.

Fowles, L. (1976). *Mass Advertising as Social Forecast: A Method for Futures Research*. Westport: Greenwood Press.

Fox, S. (1984). *The Mirror Makers*. New York: William Morrow.

Fries, P. H. (1993). Information Flow in Written Advertising. In: J. E. Alatis (ed.), *Language, Communication, and Social Meaning*, pp. 336-352. Washington, D. C.: Georgetown University Press.

Frutiger, A. (1989). *Signs and Symbols*. New York: Van Nostrand.

Goffman, E. (1979). *Gender Advertisements*. New York: Harper and Row.

Harris, R. & Seldon, A. (1962). *Advertising and the Public*. London: André Deutsch.

Hawkes, T. (1977). *Structuralism and Semiotics*. Berkeley: University of California Press.

Heighton, E. & Cunningham, D. (1976). *Advertising in the Broadcast Media*. Belmont: Wadsworth.

Heinberg, R. (1989). *Memories and Visions of Paradise*. Los Angeles: J. P. Tarcher

Hindley, D. & Hindley, G. (1972). *Advertising in Victorian England*. London: Wayland.

Hoshino, K. (1987). Product Conceptualization. In: J. Umiker-Sebeok (ed.), *Marketing and Semiotics*, pp. 41-56. Berlin: Mouton de Gruyter.

Inglis, F. (1972). *The Imagery of Power: A Critique of Advertising*. London: Heinemann.

Jakobson, R. (1960). Linguistics and Poetics. In: T. A. Sebeok (ed.), *Style and Language*, pp. 34-45. Cambridge, Mass.: MIT Press.

Jean, G. (1966). *La poésie*. Paris: Seuil.

Jhally, S. (1987). *The Codes of Advertising*. New York: St. Martin's Press.

Johnson, M. (1987). *The Body in the Mind: The Bodily Basis of Meaning, Imagination and Reason*. Chicago: University of Chicago Press.

Jung, C. G. (1957). *The Undiscovered Self*. New York: Mentor.

Key, W. B. (1972). *Subliminal Seduction*. New York: Signet.

Key, W. B. (1976). *Media Sexploitation*. New York: Signet.

Key, W. B. (1980). *The Clam-Plate Orgy*. New York: Signet.

Key, W. B. (1989). *The Age of Manipulation*. New York: Holt.

Kosslyn, S. M. (1983). *Ghosts in the Mind's Machine: Creating and Using Images in the Brain*. New York: W. W. Norton.

Krampen, M. (1991). *Children's Drawings: Iconic Coding of the Environment*. New York: Plenum.

Kubey, R. & Csikszentmihalyi, M. (1990). *Television and the Quality of Life*. Hillsdale, N. J.: Lawrence Erlbaum Associates.

Lakoff, G. & Johnson, M. (1980). *Metaphors We Live By*. Chicago: University of Chicago Press.

Lakoff, G. (1987). *Women, Fire, and Dangerous Things: What Categories Reveal about the Mind*. Chicago: University of Chicago Press.

Langer, S. (1948). *Philosophy in a New Key*. Cambridge: Harvard University Press.

Lefebvre, H. (1968). *La vie quotidienne dans le monde moderne*. Paris: Gallimard.

Leiss, W., Kline, S. & Jhally, S. (1990). *Social Communication in Advertising: Persons, Products & Images of Well-Being*. Toronto: Nelson.

Leymore, V. (1975). *Hidden Myth: Structure and Symbolism in Advertising*. London: Heinemann.

MacCannell, D. & MacCannell, J. F. (1982). *The Time of the Sign: A Semiotic Interpretation of Modern Culture*. Bloomington: Indiana University Press.

Marchand, R. (1985). *Advertising the American Dream.: Making the Way for Modernity, 1920-1940*. Berkeley: University of California Press.

McCracken, G. (1988). *Culture and Consumption*. Bloomington: Indiana University Press.

McLuhan, M. (1962). *The Gutenberg Galaxy*. Toronto: University of Toronto Press.

McLuhan, M. (1964). *Understanding Media*. London: Routledge & Kegan Paul.

McNeill, D. (1992). *Hand and Mind: What Gestures Reveal about Thought*. Chicago: University of Chicago Press.

Moog, C. (1990). *Are They Selling Her Lips? Advertising and Identity*. New York: Morrow.

Nöth, W. (1990). *Handbook of Semiotics.* Bloomington: Indiana University Press.

Ogden, C. K. & Richards, I. A. (1923). *The Meaning of Meaning.* London: Routledge and Kegan Paul.

Packard, V. (1957). *The Hidden Persuaders.* New York: McKay.

Panati, C. (1984). *Browser's Book of Beginnings.* Boston Houghton Mifflin.

Peirce, C. S. (1958). *Collected Papers.* Cambridge, Mass.: Harvard University Press.

Perron, P. & Danesi, M. (1993). *A. J. Greimas and Narrative Cognition.* Toronto: Soleil Publishing (Monograph Series of the Toronto Semiotic Circle, Volume 11).

Pollay, R. W. (1979). *Information Sources in Advertising History.* Westport: Greenwood.

Pollio, H., Barlow, J. Fine, H. & Pollio, M. (1977). *The Poetics of Growth: Figurative Language in Psychology, Psychotherapy, and Education.* Hillsdale, N. J.: Lawrence Erlbaum Associates.

Pope, D. (1983). *The Making of Modern Advertising.* New York: Basic.

Presbrey, F. (1968). *The History and Development of Advertising.* Westport: Greenwood.

Richards, I. A. (1936). *The Philosophy of Rhetoric.* Oxford: Oxford University Press.

Rotzoll, K., Haefner, J. & Sandage, C. (1976). *Advertising and Society: Perspectives towards Understanding.* Columbus: Copywright Grid.

Saussure, F. de (1916/1966). *Course in General Linguistics.* Paris: Payot.

Schank, R. (1984). *The Cognitive Computer.* Reading, Mass.: Addison-Wesley.

Schleidt, M. (1980). Personal Odor and Nonverbal Communication. *Ethology and Sociobiology* 1: 225-231.

Schudson, M. (1984). *Advertising: The Uneasy Persuasion.* New York: Basic.

Sebeok, T. A. (1976). *Contributions to the Doctrine of Signs.* Lanham: University Press of America.

Sebeok, T. A. (1979). *The Sign and Its Masters.* Austin: University of Texas Press.

Sebeok, T. A. (1981). *The Play of Musement.* Bloomington: Indiana University Press.

Sebeok, T. A. (1985). Pandora's Box: How and Why to Communicate 10,000 Years into the Future. In: M. Blonsky (ed.), *On Signs,* pp. 448-466. Baltimore: Johns Hopkins University Press.

Sebeok, T. A. (1986). *I Think I Am a Verb: More Contributions to the Doctrine of Signs.* New York: Plenum.

Sebeok, T. A. (1991). *A Sign is Just a Sign.* Bloomington: Indiana University Press.

Sinclair, J. (1987). *Images Incorporated: Advertising as Industry and Ideology.* Beckenham: Croom Helm.

Singer, B. (1986). *Advertising and Society*. Toronto: Addison-Wesley.

Solomon, J. (1988). *The Signs of Our Time*. Los Angeles: Jeremy P. Tarcher.

Sorgem, Y. K. (1991). Ad Games: Postmodern Conditions of Advertising. *Marketing Signs* 11: 1-15.

Spitzer, L. (1978). La publicité américaine comme art populaire. *Critique* 35: 152-171.

Umiker-Sebeok, J. (1987) (ed.). *Marketing Signs: New Directions in the Study of Signs for Sale*. Berlin: Mouton.

Umiker-Sebeok, J. (1989). Bibliography on Semiotic Approaches to Marketing. *Marketing Signs* 5/6: 1-19.

Umiker-Sebeok, J., Cossette, C., & Bachand, D. (1988). Selected Bibliography on the Semiotics of Marketing. *Semiotic Inquiry* 8: 415-423.

Vardar, N. (1992). *Global Advertising: Rhyme or Reason?* London: Chapman.

Verene, D. P. (1981). *Vico's Science of Imagination*. Ithaca: Cornell University Press.

Vestergaard, T. & Schrøder, K. (1985). *The Language of Advertising*. London: Blackwell.

Vygotsky, L. S. (1961). *Thought and Language*. Cambridge, Mass.: MIT Press.

Wernick, A. (1991). *Promotional Culture: Advertising, Ideology, and Symbolic Expression*. London: Gage.

Wheelwright, P. (1954). *The Burning Fountain: A Study in the Language of Symbolism*. Bloomington: Indiana University Press.

Williamson, J. (1985). *Decoding Advertisements: Ideology and Meaning in Advertising*. London: Marion Boyars.

Wolfe, O. (1989). Sociosemiology and Cross-Cultural Branding Strategies. *Marketing Signs* 3: 3-10.

Woodward, G. C. & Denton, R. E. (1988). *Persuasion & Influence in American Life*. Prospect Heights, Ill.: Waveland.

GLOSSARY OF TECHNICAL TERMS

Addressee   the receiver of a message; the individual or groups of individuals to whom an (advertising) message is directed

Addresser   the sender of a message; the creator of an (advertisement) text

Advertising   (from medieval Latin *advertere* "to direct one's attention to") any type or form of public announcement designed to promote the sale of specific commodities or services

Aesthesia   the ability to experience sensation; in art appreciation it refers to the fact that our senses and feelings are stimulated by the art form

Alliteration   the repetition of the initial consonant sounds or features of words

Anchorage   Roland Barthes' notion that visual images in advertisements are polysemous (having many meanings) which are, however, *anchored* to particular meaning domains by specific interpreters

Brand image   the creation of a personality for the product: i.e. the intentional creation of a product's name, packaging, price, and advertising style in order to create a recognizable personality for the product that is meant to appeal to specific consumers

Channel   the physical means by which a signal or message is transmitted

Code   the system in which signs are organized and which determines how they relate to each other to make meaningful texts

Communication   social interaction through messages; the production and exchange of messages and meanings; the use of specific modes and media of sign-making to transmit feeling-states and messages

Conative   a communicative function that describes the effect of the (advertising) message on the addressee (receiver, audience)

Concept   a connection made by the human mind (within a cultural context)

Connotation   the extended or secondary meaning of a sign; the symbolic or mythic implications of certain signifiers

Consumer advertising   advertising directed toward the promotion of some product

Contact   Roman Jakobson's term for the physical channel employed in communication and the psychological con-

	nections between addresser (sender) and addressee (receiver)
Context	the environment (physical and social) in which signs are produced and messages generated
Decoding	the process of deciphering the message inherent in a code
Deixis	the process of locating beings, objects, and events in space through signs
Denotation	the primary meaning of a sign
Emotive	a communicative function that describes the relation of the message to the addresser (sender)
Encoding	the process of putting a message together in terms of a specific code
Event fabrication effect	the term used in this book to refer to the fact that advertising texts induce in their viewers the perception that some ordinary happening (a kiss, a glance, etc.) constitutes a momentous event
Ground	the part of a metaphor that generates its meaning
Hermeneutics	the science or art of interpretation
Icon	a sign which has a direct (nonarbitrary) connection to a referent
Id	Sigmund Freud's term for the unconscious part of the psyche actuated by fundamental impulses toward fulfilling instinctual needs
Image schem	the term used by George Lakoff and Mark Johnson to refer to the recurring structures of, or in, our perceptual interactions, bodily experiences, and cognitive operations that portray locations, movements, shapes, etc. in the mind
Index	a sign that has an existential connection to a referent (indicating that something or someone is located somewhere)
Information compression effect	the term used in this book to refer to the fact that advertising presents personages, events, and information globally and instantly leaving little time for reflection on the topics, implications, words, etc. contained in an ad text, thus leading to a state by which information is desired and understood mainly in a "compressed" form
Interpretant	the process of adapting a sign's meaning in terms of personal and social experience
Intertextuality	the allusion within a text to some other text that the interpreter/receiver would have access to or knowledge of

Medium	the technical or physical means by which a message is transmitted
Message	any meaningful text produced with signs belonging to a specific code (or codes)
Metalingual	the communicative function by which the code being used is identified
Metaphor	the signifying process by which two signifying domains *(A, B)* are connected *(A is B)* explicitly or implicitly
Metonymy	the signifying process by which an entity is used to refer to another that is related to it
Mimesis	the conscious acquisition and use (imitation, emulation, etc.) of signifying structures
Model	the result of the process of taking in and *re*-forming in the mind the *in*-formation emanating from our sensorial an affective responses to the world
Myth	any story or narrative in early cultures that aims to explain the origin of something or someone
Mythologizing effect	the term used in this book to refer to the fact that advertising imbues its characters (models in ads and commercials) with a mythological aura
Mythology	the study of myths, or the creation of mythic connotations associated with some person or event
Narrative mode	the use of narrativity as the cognitive means by which something is conceptualized and then expressed — "narrated" — in verbal and/or nonverbal ways
Narrative	something narrated, told or written, such as an account, story, tale, and even scientific theory
Narrativity	the innate human capacity to produce and comprehend narratives
Object	a synonym for referent or signified; what is referred to in signification
Onomatopoeia	the iconic feature of words by which they represent a referent imitating one or several of its audio-oral properties *(drip, boom,* etc.)
Opposition	the process by which signs are differentiated through a minimal change in their form (signifier)
Osmosis	the unconscious acquisition of signifying structures in relation to environmental input
Paradigmatic	a structural relation between signs that keeps them distinct and therefore recognizable
Parallelism	the repetition of linguistic patterns (sentences, phrases, etc.)
Percept	a unit of perception (a stimulus that has been received and recognized); an immediate unit of knowing derived from sensation or feeling

Phatic	the communicative function by which contact between addresser (sender) and addressee (receiver) is established
Poetic	the communicative function based on a poetic language (metaphorical, rhythmic, etc.)
Positioning	the placing or targeting of a product for the right people
Postmodernism	the contemporary state of mind which believes that all knowledge is relative and human-made, and that there is no purpose to life beyond the immediate and the present
Propaganda	any systematic dissemination of doctrines, views, etc. reflecting specific interests and ideologies (political, social, and so on)
Public relations	the activities and techniques used by organizations and individuals to establish favorable attitudes and responses in their behalf on the part of the general public or of special groups
Publicity	the craft of disseminating any information that concerns a person, group, event, or product through some form of public media
Receiver	the one who decodes a message (the addressee)
Referent	what is referred to (any object, being, idea, or event in the world)
Referential	the communicative function by which a straightforward transmission is intended
Representamen	Charles S. Peirce's term for signifier
Representation	the process by which referents are designated by signs
Rhetoric	the study of the techniques used in all kinds of discourses, from common conversation to poetry
Semiology	Ferdinand de Saussure's term for the study of signs, now restricted, by and large, to the study of verbal signs
Semiosis	the comprehension and production of signs
Semiotics	the science or doctrine that studies signs
Sender	the transmitter or addresser of a message
Sign	something that stands for something (someone) else in some capacity
Signal	any transmission of biologically-based responses to stimuli; in communication systems it refers to the physical form of a message
Signification	the process of generating meaning through the use of signs
Signified	that part of a sign that is referred to; a synonym for referent and object

Signifier	that part of a sign that does the referring; the physical part of a sign
Structure	any repeatable or predictable aspect of signs, codes, and messages
Subtext	a text (message) implied by connotation within a text
Symbol	a sign that has an arbitrary (conventional) connection with a referent
Synecdoche	the signifying process by which a part stands for the whole
Synesthesia	the evocation of one sense modality (e.g. vision) by means of some other (e.g. hearing); the juxtaposition of sense modalities (e.g. *loud colors*)
Syntagmatic	the structural relation that combines signs in code-dependent ways
Tautology	a statement that is meaningless but enunciated as necessarily true
Tenor	the subject of a metaphor; a synonym for topic
Text	the actual message with its particular form and contents
Topic	the subject of a metaphor (a synonym for tenor)
Trade advertising	advertising that is directed toward dealers and professionals through appropriate trade publications and media
Trope	figure of speech; figurative language generally
Vehicle	the part of a metaphor to which a tenor is connected; the part that makes a concrete statement about the tenor